JOSEPH A. FITZMYER, S.J.

A Christological Catechism

New Testament Answers

PAULIST PRESS New York/Ramsey

IMPRIMI POTEST
Josephus P. Whelan, S.J.
Praepositus Provinciae Marylandiae

NIHIL OBSTAT
Reverend Joseph N. Tylenda, S.J.
Censor Deputatus

IMPRIMATUR
Rev. Msgr. John F. Donoghue
Vicar General for the Archdiocese of Washington

October 15, 1981

Library of Congress
Catalog Card Number: 82-80160

ISBN: 0-8091-2453-X

Published by Paulist Press
545 Island Road, Ramsey, N.J. 07446

Printed and bound in the
United States of America

CONTENTS

Contents

ABBREVIATIONS

AAS	Acta apostolicae sedis		Sacram Scripturam spectantia auctoritate Pontificiae Commissionis de re biblica edita (2d ed.; Naples: M. d'Auria; Rome: A. Arnodo, 1954; 3d ed., 1956)
AER	American Ecclesiastical Review		
Ang	Angelicum		
Anton	Antonianum		
ASS	Acta sanctae sedis		
BenMon	Benediktinische Monatschrift		
		HeyJ	Heythrop Journal
BeO	Bibbia e oriente	HPR	Homiletic and Pastoral Review
BKirche	Bibel und Kirche		
BLit	Bibel und Liturgie	HTR	Harvard Theological Review
BZ	Biblische Zeitschrift		
CBQ	Catholic Biblical Quarterly	IER	Irish Ecclesiastical Record
ChicStud	Chicago Studies	ITQ	Irish Theological Quarterly
CivC	Civiltà cattolica		
CJT	Canadian Journal of Theology	JBC	Jerome Biblical Commentary (ed. R. E. Brown, et al.; Englewood Cliffs, N.J.: Prentice-Hall, 1968).
ColBG	Collationes brugenses et gandavenses		
CSEL	Corpus scriptorum ecclesiasticorum latinorum		
DaS	Divino afflante Spiritu	LTK	Lexikon für Theologie und Kirche (11 vols.; 2d ed.; ed. J. Höfer and K. Rahner; Freiburg im B.: Herder, 1957–67)
DBSup	Dictionnaire de la Bible (F. Vigouroux et al.), Supplément (Paris-Letouzey et Ané, 1928–)		
DS	H. Denzinger and A. Schönmetzer, Enchiridion symbolorum (33d ed.; Freiburg im B.: Herder, 1965)	Nestle-Aland[26]	E. and E. Nestle and K. Aland, Novum Testamentum graece (26th ed.; Stuttgart: Deutsche Bibelstiftung, 1979)
		NRT	Nouvelle revue théologique
EnchBib	Enchiridion biblicum: Documenta ecclesiastica	ns	new series

OssRom	*Osservatore romano*		*mission* (7th ed.; St.
pace	with all due respect to		Meinrad, Ind.: Grail,
	the opinion(s) of . . .		1962)
PG	*Patrologia graeca* (ed. J.	*SalTer*	*Sal terrae*
	Migne)	*SBLMS*	*Society of Biblical Litera-*
PL	*Patrologia latina* (ed. J.		*ture Monograph Series*
	Migne)	*ScCatt*	*Scuola cattolica*
RB	*Revue biblique*	*Scr*	*Scripture*
RDiocNam	*Revue diocésaine de Na-*	*SdZ*	*Stimmen der Zeit*
	mur	*TBT*	*The Bible Today*
RevistB	*Revista bíblica* (Argenti-	*TheolGeg*	*Theologie der Gegenwart*
	na)	*TPQ*	*Theologisch-praktische*
RSS	*Rome and the Study of*		*Quartalschrift*
	Scripture: A Collection of	*TRev*	*Theologische Revue*
	Papal Enactments on the	*TS*	*Theological Studies*
	Study of Holy Scripture	*ZAW*	*Zeitschrift für die alttes-*
	Together with the Deci-		*tamentliche Wissenschaft*
	sions of the Biblical Com-		

Praesidi magistrisque
Collegii Sanctae Crucis Vigorniensis
summo honore Litterarum Doctoris A.D. MCMLXXIX accepto

et

praesidi magistrisque
Universitatis Scrantoniensis
summo honore Doctoris Litterarum Humaniorum eodem anno
accepto
grato animo dedicatum

FOREWORD

A few years ago the director of *Chicago Studies* asked me to prepare a brief survey of New Testament christological problems for his "Pastoral Guide to the Bible."[1] It was simply entitled "Jesus the Lord" and proposed succinct answers to fifteen questions which the director had sent to me.

The entire pastoral guide was eventually translated into Italian under the title *Catechismo biblico*.[2] Later on, the director of *La Nouvelle Revue Théologique* requested that the article be updated and revised for a French version, to which I was happy to accede.[3] The French form of the article included a further question (§14) and the reformulation of some answers to the original questions.

The text which is presented here is a further improvement of the original English article. The wording of the answers has been revised at times, and four new questions (§3, 8, 9, 10) have been added, bringing the total to 20. These new questions have been suggested to me by readers of the French form of the article.

The answer to one new question (§3), however, touches on an issue which lies at the heart of the problems discussed in this New Testament christological catechism. For the catechism builds upon the Instruction of the Biblical Commission issued in 1964 on the his-

---

1. *ChicStud* 17 (1978) 75–104.
2. Ed. George J. Dyer (Brescia: Queriniana, 1979).
3. "Nouveau Testament et christologie: Questions actuelles," *NRT* 103 (1981) 18–47, 187–208. This form of the article has appeared in Danish in *Magasin* 4-5 (1981) 3-66; an abridgement of it is also to appear in *TheolGeg* (1982).

torical truth of the Gospels. Having written a commentary on that Instruction in the year that it was issued,[4] I realize today how pertinent that Church document is to the present christological discussion. As a result, I am including in the appendix to this book a revised form of that commentary, a slightly revised form of the translation of the Instruction which I prepared in 1964, and the significant paragraph 19 of *Dei Verbum,* the apostolic constitution on Divine Revelation from Vatican Council II, which made explicit use of the Instruction. In this way it will be seen that the answers given in this catechism to the questions proposed to me have been inspired by the work of the Biblical Commission and of the fathers of Vatican Council II.

If I stress this last point, it is to clarify what I am about in this book. A moment's reflection will make it clear that tomes could be written in answer to each of the questions put to me. Originally, my intention was—and it still is—to give a *succinct,* well-worked-out answer to each question, with a minimum of bibliographic references and within a limited amount of space. Readers are asked to take this feature into account and realize the implications of such a brief-answer format. The answers are frankly proposed as my own, but they are fashioned from the standpoint of modern New Testament study and of today's research. In this regard they have been especially guided by the Instruction of the Biblical Commission.

---

4. Entitled, "The Biblical Commission's Instruction on the Historical Truth of the Gospels," *TS* 25 (1964) 386–408. A more popular discussion of the Instruction was published under the title, "The Gospel Truth: What the Recent Vatican Statement Means to Modern Catholic Biblical Scholars," *America* 110 (1964) 844–46. The *TS* article was eventually published as a pamphlet, *The Historical Truth of the Gospels (The 1964 Instruction of the Biblical Commission): With Commentary* (Glen Rock, N.J.: Paulist Press, 1965). The two articles (from *TS* and *America*) were combined into a booklet in a German version, *Die Wahrheit der Evangelien* (Stuttgart: Katholisches Bibelwerk, 1965). It was chosen to be the No. 1 issue of a series which has recently reached the hundred mark, "Stuttgarter Bibelstudien." Additions made to that form of the article have been incorporated into the revision presented in the appendix.

My intention, then, is to set forth the *New Testament data* as succinctly as I can. The limitation of the answers to such data implies no judgment about the endeavors of others, either of the magisterium, or of systematic theologians, or of patristic scholars, who might seek to answer the same questions about Jesus the Lord on the basis of other data. In this regard the reader, after having read this book, would do well to peruse the Declaration of the Sacred Congregation for the Doctrine of the Faith, *Mysterium Filii Dei,* on the Incarnation and the Blessed Trinity,[5] and above all the International Theological Commission's *Select Questions on Christology.*[6] In these two texts one will see how theologians, coping with data derived from beyond the New Testament, try to answer some similar questions. The most crucial question in this whole area of christology will always remain that about the consciousness of the historical Jesus of Nazareth. The treatment of that question by the Theological Commission is highly significant.[7] It goes beyond the purpose of this book, however, to try to deal with it in detail, but comments will be made about it in various ways, as occasion offers.

It remains to express my thanks to various persons who have helped me in bringing this book to its completion. I am indebted, first of all, to the Rev. George J. Dyer, the director of *Chicago Studies,* who initially asked me to compose such answers to his questions in the Pastoral Guide and who has granted permission for this revision and expansion of the article. Second, to Dr. John J. Collins of

---

5. See *AAS* 64 (1972) 237–41. An English translation of the Declaration can be found in *Origins* 1/2 (1972) 665–68; see also "Safeguarding Belief in the Incarnation and Trinity," *Catholic Mind* (June 1972) 61–64.

6. (Washington, D.C.: United States Catholic Conference, 1980). The Latin text can be found in *Gregorianum* 61 (1980) 609–32.

7. No attempt is made in this document to discuss the consciousness of the historical Jesus in the part of it that deals with the "knowledge of the person and work of Jesus Christ" (IA or IB); it is found rather in the section which develops "the teachings of the Council of Chalcedon and Constantinople III" (IIID), specifically in §6.1ff. The latter makes all sorts of references to the New Testament, but they are made from the systematic point of view.

DePaul University, who—as I learned only subsequently—had no small hand in the formation of the fifteen questions originally proposed. Third, to R. P. Bruno Clarot, S.J., who first brought the *Chicago Studies* article to the attention of the director of *NRT.* Fourth, to R. P. H. Jacobs, S.J., the director of *NRT,* who requested the revision of the text and thus provided the stimulus for further work on it (as well as to his translator). Fifth, to Raymond E. Brown, S.S., who was kind enough to send me comments on the revised form of the article. Lastly, to Lawrence E. Boadt, C.S.P. and other members of Paulist Press, who have graciously accepted this revision of several articles and made it into a book for me.

QUESTIONS

1. Do the Gospel Stories Present an Accurate Factual Account of the Teaching and Deeds of Jesus of Nazareth?

The question is complicated, for it is asked by implication from the viewpoint of modern historical thinking (e.g., of the sort that would ask whether Julius Caesar really crossed the Rubicon or George Washington the Delaware River). From that point of view the only answer which can be given to the question is meager indeed.

a. The main reason for such an answer is that we have inherited in the New Testament four different stories which purport to tell us what Jesus said and did. Though they contain many details in which one finds agreement among them, there is also a considerable amount of disagreement. The differences between the Synoptic Gospels—Mark, Matthew, and Luke—and the Johannine Gospel are notorious (e.g., Did Jesus go up to Jerusalem during his ministry only once, or several times? Was he put to death on Passover or on the eve of Passover?). The Johannine Gospel has been clearly composed with a preoccupation that is not that of the question posed above, for its stated purpose is: "These things are written that you may *believe* that Jesus is the Christ, the Son of God, and that believing you *may have life in his name*" (20:31). Moreover, the Jesus of John's Gospel does not speak as does the Jesus of the Synoptics—the former uses long, solemn discourses, filled with symbolic language, "I am" formulas, and references to the Father, and has virtually no parables. Very few of the episodes of Jesus' ministry recorded in the Fourth Gospel parallel those of the Synoptics. Apart from the account of Jesus' initial relation to John the Baptist (which itself differs in crucial details [cf. John 3:26; 4:2]), the cure of the son of a royal official in Capernaum (4:46–53), the multiplication of the loaves (6:5–13), the walking on the waters (6:16–21), and a few scattered details of lesser moment, there is scarcely any real parallelism in the Johannine account with the Synoptics before the last days of Jesus in Jerusalem. (What a picture of Jesus we would have, if we had only the Fourth Gospel!)

b. Within the Synoptic tradition itself there are many similarities, which one might be tempted to regard as the factual core. But here, too, there are numerous differences, and not a few of the divergences are of great significance when one inquires about an "accurate factual account." To cite but a few examples: There are the different stories in the infancy narratives of Matthew and Luke that defy harmonization; in the former the heavenly communication about the child to be born is made to Joseph, but in the latter to Mary. One cannot claim without further ado that it actually came to both of them! Again, how different are the stories in Matthew 2 from those in Luke 2. Consider the divergent form of Jesus' sayings about the prohibition of divorce (with or without an exception), the number of petitions in the Our Father (seven in the Matthean form, five in the Lucan), the number of beatitudes at the beginning of the Sermon on the Mount/Plain (eight in Matthew, four in Luke), the problematic ending of Mark's Gospel, which may have ended at 16:8, with an account of the empty tomb, but with no appearances of the risen Christ. The upshot is that, when one considers the Synoptic Gospel stories from the viewpoint of accurate, factual recounting, they can scarcely be judged to be prime examples of such writing.

c. If one were to try to limit the actual account of what Jesus did and said to what is found to be in agreement in the four Gospels, there are still problems. On the one hand, this would for the most part limit the discussion to the substance of the passion narratives (Jesus' "Last Supper" with his followers, his arrest, the crucifixion, death, and burial of Jesus, and the finding of the empty tomb). On the other hand, with the exception of a few other episodes in the ministry itself (e.g., Peter's confession of Jesus [recounted, indeed, in different forms; see §9 below]), the vast majority of the Jesus-tradition would be seen to be reflected in a form that is at once concordant and discordant.

d. Furthermore, the concordant similarity in the Synoptic accounts of Jesus' ministry raises a further question about the independence of these reports one from the other—and then whether they are any more accurate or reliable than the Johannine account. No matter what theoretic solution one uses for the Synoptic problem (the discordant concord of the Gospels of Mark, Matthew, and Luke), there is scarcely anyone today who would deny the interdependence of the Marcan, Matthean, and Lucan Gospels.

The most commonly used solution to the Synoptic problem is the so-called two-document hypothesis or the modified two-source theory. The two documents used in the composition of the Lucan and Matthean Gospels would have been Mark and "Q" (an abbreviation of the German word *Quelle,* "source," used to designate the Greek written source postulated for about two hundred and thirty verses common to Matthew and Luke and not found in Mark). The modified two-source theory accepts the same two sources but admits that Luke also had a private (written or oral) source, "L," and that Matthew had a similar source, "M." In either case, the dependence of the Matthean and Lucan Gospels on the Marcan is admitted for a large bulk of the common material. If one were to prefer the solution proposed by the eighteenth-century scholar J. J. Griesbach, according to which the Marcan Gospel is an abridgement of the Matthean and Lucan Gospels—a highly questionable solution—a similar dependence is at least implied. Other solutions proposed in this century by

French interpreters, such as X. Léon-Dufour and M.-E. Boismard, are not free of some form of interdependence of these Gospels.

Only a naive fundamentalism would still insist on the Synoptic Gospels as products solely of independent oral transmission. But if the Synoptic Gospels are interdependent, then the differences among them reveal that they are not all factually accurate. An editorial hand, modifying or redacting the transmitted material, has been at work on them, and for reasons other than the concern of history.

e. On the other hand, no serious New Testament interpreter today would try to maintain that the Gospel stories about Jesus are fabrications out of whole cloth (*pace* J. M. Allegro, R. Augstein, and others). An historical tradition lies behind both the Synoptics and John. The concern of the modern interpreter of these writings, however, is not so much that of sorting out how much in either tradition is factually accurate as of appreciating the heritage about Jesus that is enshrined in them.

f. The multiplicity of accounts in the early Christian heritage reveals that they were not composed for the mere purpose of recording facts about Jesus. Between the facts themselves and the composition of the accounts at least a generation of Christian preaching about him and of tradition about him, oral and written, had intervened. This preaching and tradition included a recollection of what Jesus did and said, but it could not help but be colored by hindsight, meditation, faith in him as the risen Lord, a developing christology, and echoes of later Church or Church-synagogue controversies, of missionary endeavors, and of persecution. Such phenomena do not necessarily preclude accurate reporting, but the end-products, being four in number and having different emphases, scarcely give the impression that they were intentionally written to be accurate, factual accounts. Those extrinsic factors have left at times clear traces in the accounts and contribute to the impression that they were written for quite other purposes, as even Luke 1:1–4 (with its stress on *asphaleia,* "assurance") or John 20:31 reveals.

2. How Much, in Fact, Can We Claim To Know about the Historical Jesus?

The sources of our information about the historical Jesus of Nazareth are limited. They consist of a few items in ancient extra-biblical writings, possibly some details in apocryphal gospels of later date, isolated pieces of information in the New Testament writings other than the canonical Gospels, and what may be regarded as some authentic historical traditions embedded in the canonical Gospels themselves.

a. One can almost count on the fingers of one hand the extra-biblical references to Jesus in ancient writers who are independent of the New Testament. A few lines are devoted to "Christ," the author of a "pernicious superstition," by the Roman historian Tacitus (A.D. 56[?]–116[?]), who tells of Christians related to the burning of Rome by the emperor Nero and of the execution of Christ under the "procurator" Pontius Pilate, while Tiberius was emperor (*Annales* 15.44,3).

Suetonius (A.D. 69[?]—?) further tells of the expulsion of the Jews from Rome by the emperor Claudius because of a tumult [between Jews and Jewish Christians?] instigated by "Chrestus" (probably to be understood as *Christus* because of itacism [the tendency of the time to pronounce Greek *ē* as *iota*] working in reverse) ca. A.D. 49 (*Vita Claudii* 25.4).

The *Testimonium Flavianum* in the writings of the Jewish historian, Flavius Josephus (A.D. 38–100[?]), speaks of Jesus as "a wise man, if indeed one ought to call him a man" and as one put to death by Pilate, "having heard him accused by men of the highest standing among us" (*Ant.* 18.3,3 §63–64 [written ca. A.D. 93–94]). But that testimony is widely suspected of being at least partly interpolated by Christian glossators of manuscripts of Josephus, if not wholly so. Yet another passage (*Ant.* 20.9,1 §200), scarcely interpolated, tells of the putting to death of James, "the brother of Jesus called the Christ."

Again, Pliny the Younger (A.D. 61–112) knows that Christians of his day in Bithynia (Asia Minor) chanted verses "to Christ, as if to a god" (*Christo quasi deo,* in *Ep.* 10.96,7).

Lucian of Samosata, a traveling lecturer and Sophist rhetor (A.D. 120–180[?]), writes about the death of Peregrinus, a Cynic philosopher, who became a Christian for a while before reverting to Cynicism. For a time he associated with "the priests and scribes" of the Christians of Palestine, "interpreted and explained some of their books," and was revered by them "next after that other, to be sure, whom they still worship, the man who was crucified in Palestine because he introduced this new cult into (human) life" (*De morte Peregrini* 11). Lucian also speaks of Jesus as the "first lawgiver" of the Christians who "persuaded them that they all are brothers of one another" (an allusion to Matt 23:8?) and refers to them as "worshipping that crucified sophist himself and living under his laws" (ibid., 13).

Finally, a baraita (an "outside" addition to the Mishnaic tradition) of the Babylonian Talmud (*Sanhedrin* 43a [3d cent. at the earliest]) speaks of Yeshu, who practiced magic and led Israel into apostasy, had disciples, and was "hanged on the eve of Passover."

These extra-biblical texts are problematic, at times cryptic, at times allusive, at times interpolated. Yet even when due allowance is made for such problems in them, these extra-biblical references, independent of the New Testament writings, support at most a few details known mainly from the passion narratives of the canonical Gospels: that Jesus was put to death in the reign of Tiberius under Pontius Pilate, that some leaders of the Palestinian Jews of his time were involved in his death, and that he had some followers by whom he was regarded as "Christ," lawgiver and founder of a new way of life, and "quasi deo."

b. The apocryphal *Gospel according to Thomas,* extant in a fourth-century Coptic version (see J. M. Robinson [dir.], *The Nag Hammadi Library in English* [New York: Harper & Row, 1977] 116–30) and in a few Greek fragments of the second/third century (see my *Essays on the Semitic Background of the New Testament* [London: Chapman, 1971; reprinted, Missoula, Mt.: Scholars, 1974] 355–433), ascribes to Jesus one hundred and fourteen sayings, usually introduced simply by "Jesus said." Most of these sayings, loosely strung together, actually come from a later date than that of the canonical Gospels and clearly depend on the latter. At times, their Gnostic concerns and reformulations betray the matrix in which they took shape. But this apocryphal gospel preserves some sayings or parables in a form which is more primitive than that found in the canonical Gospels—i.e., devoid of editorial additions which almost certainly reflect the concerns of the evangelists (compare logion 64 with Matt 22:1–14 and Luke 14:16–24). But does "more primitive" necessarily mean "authentic"? It is not impossible, but who can say for sure?

c. By and large, the apocryphal gospels are the outgrowth of the earlier Gospel tradition, but they are also born of other preoccupations and are marked with tendencies which emerged only later in Christian and other circles. If we have mentioned the *Gospel according to Thomas* as possibly containing some primitive tradition about Jesus, it was to single it out from the bulk of other apocryphal gospels and related writings. Many of the other apocryphal gospels are a part of Gnostic writings, indeed only a small part of these writings. The bulk of the latter do not bear the title "gospel," can only with a stretch of the imagination be regarded as "literature" in any refined sense, and stem from questionable (scarcely Christian) sources. This is true of the majority of the texts in *The Nag Hammadi Library in English* mentioned above. This has to be stressed over against the tendentious claims of some scholars to maintain that all the so-called apocryphal gospels actually contain material which is more primitive than that in the canonical Gospels. If I say this, it is not out of any prejudice in favor of the canonical Gospels, but rather because of an educated conviction about the nature of the material enshrined in the apocryphal gospels (*pace* H. Koester, *HTR* 73 [1980] 105–30, who is naive). Each passage in the apocryphal gospels would have to be scrutinized as thoroughly as passages in the canonical Gospels.

d. Within the New Testament itself, yet outside of the Gospel tradition, we find details about the earthly life and ministry of Jesus which may clearly be independent of this tradition, being composed prior to it at times. (I prescind from what is found in the Acts of the Apostles, because much of the detail in it may simply be echoing Luke's first volume.) In the genuine Pauline corpus, composed prior to the earliest Gospel (Mark), we learn not only of the primitive kerygma about Jesus' death, burial, resurrection, and appearances as risen Lord (1 Cor 15:3–5), but also about his "Last Supper" with his disciples and of the institution of the Eucharist "on the night he was betrayed" (1 Cor 11:23–25), of his "sufferings" (Phil 3:10), of his "cross" (1 Cor 1:17–18; Phil 2:8), of his "crucifixion" (Gal 2:20; 3:1; 1 Cor 1:23), of his "death" (1 Thess 5:10; 1 Cor 11:26; Rom 6:3), and of his "burial" (1 Cor 15:4; Rom 6:4). Allusion is further made to his being "hung on a tree" (Gal 3:13). In his severe indictment of his former co-religionists, Paul speaks of "the Jews who killed the Lord Jesus" (1 Thess 2:14–15). He also knows of some sayings of Jesus, about the prohibition of divorce (1 Cor 7:10–11), about the Eucharist (1 Cor 11:23–25), and about the eschaton (1 Thess 4:15).

In the possibly Deutero-Pauline Letter to the Colossians, allusion is made to Jesus being "nailed" to the cross (2:14). In the certainly Deutero-Pauline First Letter to Timothy mention is made of Jesus' appearance before Pilate (6:13). See further 1 Pet 2:24 (cf. Acts 5:30; 10:39; 13:29); Heb 6:6; 13:12. Again, what is striking in these extra-evangelical references is the amount of detail which supports mainly the passion narratives, but little of the rest of the story about Jesus (save perhaps a few of his sayings; see further D. L. Dungan, *The Sayings of Jesus in the Churches of Paul* [Philadelphia: Fortress, 1971]).

e. When one considers the things recorded in the canonical Gospels about Jesus' sayings and deeds, one has to recall what was said about these New Testament writings in §1 above: that their purpose was quite other than that of an accurate factual account. Being primarily testimonies of faith and propaganda for faith, they do not pretend to give us *per se* a factual sketch of the earthly life and ministry of Jesus of Nazareth. Nothing is really said in them about his physical appearance or his customary habits—or even about his historical consciousness. Being composed at least a generation after his death, the canonical Gospels cannot be regarded as *first-hand* evidence of his consciousness or *first-hand* reflections of his character; they are not the equivalent of tape-recordings of his words, stenographic reports of his utterances, or cinematographic reproductions of his deeds.

f. Though twentieth-century readers of the Gospels often seek to psychoanalyze the historical Jesus or to speculate about his consciousness on the basis of these accounts, they are often unaware of the problems inherent in such speculation. It would be easier to psychoanalyze Paul of Tarsus than Jesus of Nazareth, since we have at least a few authentic letters which come from him, in which certain aspects of his character shine through. But the only thing that we are told that Jesus wrote, he wrote "with his finger on the ground," probably on sand (John 8:6,8)—and the evangelist did not bother to record what it was! The one statement supposedly written of him during his lifetime, the "title" on the cross, appears with different wording in each Gospel (see Mark 15:26; Matt 27:37; Luke 23:38; John 19:19).

g. Modern interpreters of the Gospels, however, generally acknowledge that there is a group of scenes in the ministry, a group of sayings (mainly isolated logia and parables), and the nucleus of the passion story which would have to be regarded as historical. But each passage preserving these details would have to be scrutinized and examined for its possibly editorial embellishments. Negative criteria for Jesus' teaching have been widely accepted: Whatever does not stem clearly from the Old Testament or contemporary Jewish teaching or does not betray the concerns of (later) early-Church controversy, debate, or casuistry should be ascribed to him. Other criteria, less widely admitted, for judging his teaching have also been invoked: the principle of multiple, independent attestation (e.g., the Pauline and Synoptic tradition about Jesus' teaching on divorce); the nuance of his eschatologically-based demand for repentance. These criteria would tend to give us a *minimum* of his teaching—what is *necessarily* historical. But they also are not the final word of decision. For they are open to the obvious objection that one cannot rule out that Jesus actually taught what other Jewish teachers might have taught. However, they do represent the earnest attempt of sincere modern scholars to cope with the problem that the words and teaching of Jesus in the Gospels present.

h. A brief sketch of what is known of the historical Jesus might run somewhat like this. He was a Palestinian Jew, born of a woman named Mary married to a carpenter, Joseph. He lived in Nazareth of Galilee, having been born in the last days of Herod the Great (37–4 B.C.). He began a ministry of preaching and teaching about the fifteenth year of Tiberius (A.D. 28), the date given for the ministry of John the Baptist (Luke 3:1), to which his own ministry was related. Jesus' ministry was centered in Capernaum in Galilee, at least at the outset, though it was not confined there. He preached in Galilee in the tetrarchy of Herod Antipas, who had imprisoned and executed John, during the prefecture of Pontius Pilate (A.D. 26–36) and high-priesthood of Caiaphas (A.D. 18–36). The length of his ministry cannot be established with certainty, possibly a minimum of three years (determined by possible allusions to three Passovers in John 2:13,23; 6:4[?]; 11:55—but the Johannine references are scarcely meant as a complete list, and the Synoptics know of only one Passover).

As a Palestinian Jewish religious teacher, he came under the influence of contemporary Jewish religious, ethical, and apocalyptic thinking; at times he disagreed with other Jewish teachers (in his attitude toward the temple, the Mosaic law, the observance of the Sabbath, and other traditions of the Fathers; see below for some more specific themes of his preaching and teaching). His difference with other Jewish teachers manifested itself in particularly acute fashion with Pharisees, Sadducees, and others who professed to be interpreters of the Hebrew Scriptures for the people. He gathered about him a group of disciples or followers, prominent among whom were Simon bar Jonah (or John) and his brother Andrew, and two of the sons of Zebedee, John and James. Twelve of these disciples he associated closely with himself and his work, but their relationship to the rest of his followers during his ministry cannot be further determined. It is not easy to say whether or not he set down a definite way of life for them. The obvious horror repeatedly associated with the name of Judas Iscariot in New Testament recollections, "one of the Twelve" (Mark 14:10, 20,43; John 6:70–71; cf. Mark 3:14,19; Matt 10:2,4; Luke 6:13,16), eloquently testifies to the formation of the Twelve as a choice of Jesus himself in his ministry.

That ministry eventually brought him to Jerusalem, and on one occasion, about the time of Passover, he was arrested with the connivance of Judas Iscariot. Interrogated by leaders of the Jerusalem Jewish people and brought by them before Pontius Pilate, the prefect of Judea, he was condemned to death and crucified outside the city and buried the same day.

Days later, on the first day of the week, his tomb was found empty, and his followers soon reported appearances of him alive, as "raised" from the dead (1 Cor 15:4). A twofold list of witnesses of the risen Jesus is preserved in 1 Cor 15:5–7: (a) Cephas (the official first witness—see Luke 24:34), the Twelve, more than five hundred disciples; (b) James, and all the apostles.

i. To the ministry and activity of the historical Jesus the earliest New Testament writer, Paul of Tarsus, traces his "gospel," his call (Gal 1:12,16) to be an "apostle to the Gentiles" (Rom 11:13), and, by implication, his insight into Christians as the "body of Christ" (1 Cor 12:27–28). But the historical Jesus had already become for Paul "Jesus our Lord" (1 Cor 9:1).

3. Is Not Such an Approach to the Historical Jesus and to the Canonical Gospels Tantamount to an Implicit Reduction in Christian Faith and Contrary to a Centuries-Long Tradition of Gospel-Interpretation?

At first sight, it may seem so, but in the long run such an approach is the end-product of a mode of interpretation within the Christian community and the Roman Catholic Church which has been a-brewing since the Renaissance at least, when the first critical studies of the Gospels and of the New Testament began.

a. At first, these studies concerned the *text* of the Greek New Testament, when the thrust of scholarly interest within the Christian community centered on a return *ad fontes* ("back to the sources"). The debate then involved the esteem to be accorded to the ancient Greek manuscripts of the New Testament, which were gradually coming to light, over against the Latin Vulgate, on the one hand, and the better Greek manuscripts over against the *Textus Receptus* or what we call today the (inferior) Byzantine or Koine text-tradition, on the other. Today, when our critical Greek New Testament texts are based on the best ancient Greek manuscripts, we realize how primitive the critical discussion then was.

b. Later, the critical discussion concerned the nature of the Greek language in which the New Testament was written. Since it was clearly different from (some even said "inferior to") classical Greek, was it the language of the Holy Spirit, inspired and shaped for the transmission of the Christian "word of God," or was it simply written in a form of Hellenistic Greek, such as was being gradually made known with the discovery of Greek papyrus texts in Egypt?

c. At the end of the eighteenth century, the critical interpretation of the Gospels moved to source criticism, the analysis of the relation among the Synoptic Gospels, one to the other (see §1d above for the names of various theories eventually proposed).

d. At the beginning of the twentieth century, this source criticism, which had reached an impasse, gave way to form criticism, in which the units of the Synoptic tradition were studied to ascertain their (stylized) form and the history of their transmission from one Gospel to another. From this study emerged the categories of the sayings and parables of Jesus, the miracle-stories, the pronouncement-stories (narratives preserved because of the pronouncement or "punch-line" enshrined in them [see further §6 below]), and finally stories about Jesus (the narrative tradition proper).

e. Form criticism, which tended to be atomistic and to say little about the Gospels as a whole and as we have them, gave rise to two other forms of interpretation, redaction criticism and composition criticism. The former sought to study the Gospel as a whole and how the evangelist had shaped and modified the material which he had inherited for his own literary and theological purposes; the latter sought to study how the evangelist freely composed material to embellish his narrative account or collection of Jesus' sayings.

f. While these kinds of criticism (source, form, redaction, and composition criticism) were being used in the interpretation of the Gospels, there were also at work modern forms of literary criticism, which sought to analyze poetic, rhetorical, symbolical, and dramatic techniques used by the evangelists. Thus many modern tools of historical and literary interpretation came to be used in the study of the Gospels as in other types of literature.

g. This sophisticated mode of Gospel-interpretation was unknown indeed in earlier centuries of the Church and was born of the mode of studying literature inherited by twentieth-century readers from the Renaissance and Enlightenment. Today it is no little affected by the mentality formed by contemporary news media (especially that of the *New York Times*).

It is not that twentieth-century interpreters arrogantly maintain that they now have a key to the Scriptures which was lacking in former centuries. They are, however, aware that the archaeological and papyrological discoveries of the late eighteenth and nineteenth centuries have opened up bodies of literature from ancient Mesopotamia, Canaan, Egypt, Asia Minor, and Palestine, which Christians of former generations and centuries never knew. The study of the ancient texts of the Bible cannot be isolated, one now realizes, from comparable literary forms and narratives which such discoveries have brought to light—only in recent centuries in God's providence. One realizes today that the Bible is the result of a long process of growth, made up of writings comparable to literary texts of diverse ages and traditions, and that it cannot be interpreted in isolation—as if it dropped from heaven in King James English!

h. The major result of such critical study of the Gospels has been the realization that the Gospel tradition enshrines within it three sorts of material about Jesus of Nazareth. These are the three stages of the Gospel tradition with which any proper reading and study of the Gospels must cope. *First,* what Jesus of Nazareth did and said during the course of his earthly ministry in Palestine and its environs (Stage I). This would represent the stage of his *ipsissima verba* (his "very words"), including the modes which he chose to express his preaching and teaching about God, the kingdom, and himself. *Second,* what the apostles and disciples preached about him after his death (Stage II). At this stage Jesus the preacher had become the preached One, and the testimony borne to him and his mission had been suffused with faith in him as the risen Lord and Christ (Acts 2:36). The faithful explanation of his deeds and words passed on by the apostles and disciples was reproduced with what is often called "Easter-faith," i.e., with an *added* understanding and a *new* comprehension of him, his words, his deeds, and his impact as a whole, which came only with their faith in him and experience of him as the risen and glorified Lord: "His disciples did not understand this at first; but when Jesus was glorified, then they remembered that this had been written of him and had been done to him" (John 12:16; cf. 2:22). *Third,* what the evangelists wrote down about him in their various Gospels (Stage III). Pursuing a method and a goal peculiar to each, the evangelists used the tradition which had grown up about him in the preaching of Stage II. But they *selected*

material from it (sayings and parables, miracle-stories, pronouncement-stories, and stories about him, John the Baptist, and the apostles), *synthesized* it into their own literary compositions, *explicated* it
by redactional modifications and additions, and *fashioned* it all into a
unique literary form that we call "Gospel," indeed, into the four accounts which we know as the canonical Gospels.

But still other material from Stage II, the tradition of which did
not cease to grow with the composition of the canonical Gospels, re-
sulted in other Gospel-forms which the early Christian community
did not consider as authentic or "recognized" (*homologoumena,* to
use Eusebius' term for the canonical writings, *Hist. eccl.* 3.25,3).
These are the so-called apocryphal gospels. By and large, they
scarcely reflect Stage I (see §2c above).

This threefold distinction of the Gospel tradition about Jesus of
Nazareth is widely admitted today by interpreters in the Christian
tradition of various confessional backgrounds, even though all may
not use the same terminology of it.

i. In the Roman Catholic communion this mode of interpretation of the Gospels and this distinction find modern support in three
ecclesiastical texts of this century: (1) *Divino afflante Spiritu,* Pope
Pius XII's encyclical of 1943 on the Promotion of Biblical Studies,
which strongly insisted on the study of literary forms in the Bible as
the key to the interpretation of it (§35–39; *AAS* 35 [1943] 314–17;
EnchBib §558–60; *RSS,* 97–99). This insistence gave implicit encour-
agement to the use of form criticism by Roman Catholic interpreters,
even in the study of the Gospels. (2) *Instructio de historica evangeliorum veritate,* the "Instruction on the Historical Truth of the Gospels" of the Biblical Commission in 1964, which espoused outrightly
the form-critical and redaction-critical methods of interpretation of
the Gospels and made explicit use of the three stages of the tradition
mentioned above (see further the Appendix). (3) *Dei Verbum,* the
dogmatic constitution of Vatican Council II on "Divine Revelation"
(1965), which in one brief paragraph (§19) succinctly recapitulated
the teaching of the Biblical Commission's Instruction, thus making it

its own view of Gospel-interpretation (see Appendix). Hence even Church authorities have today espoused and supported the modern critical interpretation of the canonical Gospels, recognizing that in God's providence a key to the interpretation of them has indeed been given to the Christian community, which was not had earlier, which has opened up in a remarkable, undreamed-of way the treasures of these biblical writings, and which is neglected only to the detriment of Christian faith itself. Why in this age? An easy answer is to refer to the great ecumenical advances between Roman Catholics and other Christians born of the Reformation. The rapprochement which has taken place between these two historic Christian groups in the interpretation of the Bible can only be explained by reference to this mode of historical-critical interpretation of Scripture unknown earlier.

j. Finally, it should be apparent that the error in any simplistic or fundamentalist approach to the Gospels is precisely the confusing of Stage III with Stage I of the Gospel tradition. At least a generation elapsed between them, during which what was remembered about Jesus in Stage I was subject to much constructive Christian reflection born of faith in him as Christ the Lord. What the evangelists have put on the lips of Jesus is not simply his "very words" (*ipsissima verba*)—without further ado! It may well rest on something that he had said, but that "something" has to be ferreted out in each instance with form-critical and redaction-critical methods. The evangelists have given us neither a stenographic record of Jesus' words nor a cinematographic view of his deeds. What the Gospels present to us from Stage I has been filtered through the tradition of Stage II and the selective, editorial, and explicative process of Stage III. In other words, the Gospels show us how Jesus was presented to Christian readers about A.D. 65 (Mark), or about A.D. 80 (Matthew, Luke), or about A.D. 90 (John). Indirectly, they also supply us with evidence of how Jesus was preached as "Lord and Messiah" during the 30's, 40's, and 50's, and in that preaching how he was perceived to have been in his ministry ca. A.D. 30.

To pretend that Stage III equals Stage I is a form of naïveté. It can have disastrous effects eventually, as has been attested often: either intellectual suicide (a refusal to think and use God's greatest natural gift to human beings, the intellect) or a total loss of faith (a failure to follow where his Spirit guides the Christian community).

4. What Themes in the Gospels Are Accepted as Representing the Teachings of Jesus Himself?

Even though modern New Testament interpreters scrutinize every saying or teaching put on Jesus' lips by the evangelists, there is a general agreement about certain themes of his authentic teaching (recall the criteria mentioned in §2 above).

One must realize at the outset that the tradition about Jesus' ministry in both the Synoptics and John juxtaposes many teachings about God, the kingdom, salvation, sin, ethics, and eschatology without topical arrangement or systematic presentation. Moreover, no synthetic body of doctrine has been ascribed to Jesus; hence attempts to synthesize "themes" of his teaching have to be recognized for what they are—modern constructs. With this in mind, we may single out five topics as the main themes of the preaching of the historical Jesus.

a. The primary theme, both explicit in his sayings and parables and implicit in his miracles and deeds, was that a new mode of God's salvation was being offered to human beings—that Yahweh's sovereign activity was manifesting itself anew in human history, inaugurating an era when human beings would be accosted to react in faith to this divine salvific manifestation. "Salvation" as deliverance from physical evil, personal danger or sickness, national disaster, or moral degradation was offered by Yahweh to his *chosen* people of old through his spokesmen, Moses and the prophets. In the Old Testament Yahweh is often hailed by Israel as its "Savior" (Isa 43:11; 45:15,21; Hos 13:4; cf. Ps 68:19–20). But Jesus' main teaching was a proclamation of salvation which prescinded from the election of Israel, which differed at times with some elements of its legal tradition, and which called people to eschatological repentance, in a uniform mode centered in his own person (making acceptance of himself a critical issue in their lives). In him this new and final divine offer of salvation was made to all human beings, to the poor, to the outcasts, to sinners, perhaps even to Samaritans, and non-Jews who would come to him (depending, indeed, on how one assesses the Gospel tradition about Jesus' dealings with non-Jews and Samaritans). (For a more specific form of this salvific teaching, see the answer to question 5.)

b. A second theme of Jesus' preaching was the fundamental validity of what Scripture and tradition of old had taught. Jesus repeated the *Shema* (Deut 6:4, quoted in Mark 12:29) and acknowledged the law in the Old Testament as the source of God's will for human conduct. But he also displayed a new way of allowing it to shape human life and conduct, apart from all casuistry. Not all of Jesus' opposition to the interpretations of the scribes and Pharisees recorded in the canonical Gospels can be ascribed to later Church-synagogue disputes (see Mark 7:6–7). Related to this fundamental regard for the past is his attitude toward the older forms of piety (prayer, fasting, and almsgiving, Matt 6:1–18) and toward the observance of the sabbath or cultic worship (Mark 2:23–27). But he also insisted on the true and spiritual meaning of such practices and sought to purify them of all too-human attitudes (evasion, hypocrisy, pride) which easily became associated with beliefs and traditions of old.

c. A third theme of Jesus' preaching was a special emphasis on God as Father. His preaching reinforced the traditional Israelite view of God without introducing great novelties into the general picture. Yahweh was still the sole divine being who chose Israel, who gave it the law, and judged all mankind; his activity was still ruling human existence, guiding all things in its providence. Yahweh was, indeed, the father of Israel (see Deut 32:6; Jer 3:4,19; 31:9; Isa 63:16). But Jesus regarded Yahweh as Father in a special way, calling him "Abba" with an individual, personal nuance (Mark 14:36) and teaching his followers to acknowledge that fatherhood in a new way in prayer (Matt 6:9–13; Luke 11:2–4). This emphasis on God as Father is presented differently in the Synoptic and Johannine traditions. In the latter it is a full-blown development. But it is a theme of teaching which in its primitive form is to be traced to Jesus himself.

d. A fourth theme of Jesus' teaching implicitly involved his own person and the role which he was to play in God's new form of salvation. He acted as an agent of Yahweh, as one who could forgive sins and could reinterpret God's word in Scripture. Moreover, he coped constantly with the presence of sin in human beings, teaching that God's forgiveness was available for it—precisely through himself. An aspect of his mission can be seen in his willingness to differ with the legal attitudes of old and some widespread beliefs and customs rooted in the Old Testament itself (e.g., his attitude toward adultery [Matt 5:27] and divorce [Mark 10:2–12; Luke 16:18]). Thus, the stance he assumed vis-à-vis Moses, the Scriptures, and God revealed much about himself. But it was only an implicit and indirect teaching. Yet the impact which his teaching, his ministry, and his personality made on those who heard him caused many of them to realize that he was presenting himself as someone other than the rest of contemporary teachers and prophets of old (Mark 1:22).

e. Finally, his teaching included a new emphasis on the role of love in human life. The Old Testament had insisted on the love of God and the love of one's neighbor (= one's fellow Jew—Deut 6:4–5; Lev 19:18). Jesus not only reiterated that insistence (Mark 12:30–31), but extended it to include even one's enemies (Matt 5:44) and saw in it the summation of all that was demanded of the pious Israelite (Matt 22:40) and the interiorization of obedience itself. This attitude was at the root of all other specific demands (about wealth and the poor, about taxes and Rome, about food or drink and sinners). The Johannine tradition reformulated it in its own way and with its own emphasis, "In this will all know that you are my disciples, if you have love for one another" (John 13:35).

Some modern interpreters might be inclined to contest one or other item in the above list, but that merely indicates the difficulty that faces one in trying to isolate themes of teaching that seem to go back to the historical Jesus himself. The themes listed above are formulated in one way or another in the various Gospel traditions, even though not all the possible references for them have been supplied.

5. What Did Jesus Teach about the Kingdom of God?

The kingship of God is a widely used Old Testament notion, even though the exact expression, "kingdom of God," which is so common in one form or another in the New Testament, is rarely found in the protocanonical writings of the Old Testament. The closest form is *malkût Yahweh,* "the kingdom of the Lord" (in post-exilic 1 Chr 28:5; cf. deuterocanonical Wisd 10:10).

a. The kingship of God was a way of expressing Yahweh's sovereignty over his human creatures, indeed over all of creation. His kingship denoted a right to be acknowledged as having a dominant influence in the lives of human creatures (see Ps 22:28; 45:6; 103:19; 145:11,13; Dan 4:3,34; 1 Chr 17:14; 29:11). This kingly influence was understood above all as "salvific" (see §4 above), but it was also advisory (for he was to be consulted oracularly, in the temple), judicatory (for he was to pass judgment on human and national conduct), and covenantal (for his activity was governed by his sovereign attributes of loving kindness [*ḥesed*], righteousness (*ṣedeq, ṣedāqāh*], fidelity [*'emet*], and mercy [*raḥāmîm*]). Especially in the post-exilic period Yahweh's kingly activity developed an eschatological aspect, associating it with the "day of the Lord." This development introduced a temporal aspect which promised not only a new intervention of God in human affairs, but also the expectation of a manifestation of his sovereign rule with the establishment of peace, bounty, and harmony for all who would acknowledge his dominion (see Isa 2:2–

4; 11:6–9; Mic 4:1–4; described with apocalyptic stage-props in Isa 24–27; Zech 9–14).

b. The "kingdom of God" (or "of heaven") in Jesus' preaching was a specific way in which he announced the new form of God's salvation. Though there are Qumran expressions which echo the Old Testament's teaching about Yahweh's "kingship" (1QM 12:7; 4QEn-Giants[a] 9:6; etc.), the expression "kingdom of God" or "of heaven" has scarcely been found in these texts. Hence one may ask about how frequently it was used in contemporary Palestinian Jewish usage. The emphasis that it receives in Jesus' teaching in the canonical Gospels is, therefore, significant. Yet what is striking is that Jesus rarely explained what God's kingdom or kingship meant, more or less taking it for granted that it would be understood. The salvific and temporal (eschatological) aspects of that kingship were stressed, but one notes that in his teaching the kingdom also had a spatial aspect—for one could "enter" it (Mark 9:47; 10:23–25); it could also be "inherited" (Matt 25:34). Apocalyptic stage-props were sometimes used in the preaching of the kingdom so that it could be understood as a sort of visibly manifested irruption of God's rule on a cosmic scale. Such an apocalyptic view of the kingdom helped to prevent a naive understanding of it, as if it were a mere inward reality, an attitude of the human heart. The parables of Jesus—when divested of later ecclesiastical accretions—often presented the kingdom as a reality of God's activity among human beings; it was to grow among them, spread mysteriously, silently, but assuredly, and thus "come" into its own. The success of the kingdom was assured, even though evil might appear among its effects (but not as *its* effect).

c. The major problem in the teaching of Jesus about the kingdom is its eschatology. Are we to understand that Jesus taught that the "coming" of the kingdom in time was imminent? Here New Testament interpreters show no agreement; there are almost as many answers to this question as there are heads that think about it. The eschatology has been called "realized" (C. H. Dodd), i.e., the kingdom is already at hand in the person of Jesus. Others view it as "futurist, but near" (A. Schweitzer, R. Bultmann), i.e., expected as an imminent inbreaking, and still others as "inaugurated" (J. Jeremias), i.e., in the process of being realized, or both present and future (W. G. Kümmel). The difficulty here is that the data in the Gospel traditions are such that one cannot fit everything into one simple classification. Indeed, a writer like Luke has manifestly reformulated some of the sayings because of the delay of the parousia. The view of either Kümmel or Jeremias seems preferable, because the sayings attributed to Jesus on this point reflect the Old Testament spectrum about the "day of the Lord" itself. In reality, one cannot be certain about what Jesus of Nazareth might have said about the imminence of the kingdom.

d. In the Synoptics Jesus announces a new form of this kingly activity of God among human beings. In the Lucan Gospel he is the kingdom-preacher par excellence, whereas in the Marcan and Matthean Gospels he is rather presented as the one who establishes this kingship among human beings both in his word and in his power. (See Mark 1:14–15; Matt 12:28; note that in the Lucan Gospel John the Baptist is not a kingdom-preacher.) The "kingdom" is promised to the "saints" in Dan 7:18 (= corporate Israel); the Matthean Jesus claims for himself the authority of such a kingdom (Matt 28:18; cf. 16:28), and in the name of all the power that is thus associated with it, he commissions his followers to go forth, make disciples, baptize, and teach in his name (compare the Marcan appendix, 16:15). At the end of both the Matthean and the Marcan Gospels one sees how Jesus' preaching of the kingdom was given a very specific reformulation in later decades of the early Church.

e. Finally, in some places of the New Testament there is reference to Jesus' own kingdom (e.g., Luke 23:42; John 18:36–37; Col 1:13). It is not easy to say to what extent this notion of Jesus' own kingdom is primitive, derived from his teaching; it seems rather to have been born of a more developed christology (cf. 1 Cor 15:24–28) or of a reflection about the relationship of the Church (the kingdom of the Son) to the kingdom of God.

6. How Do Contemporary New Testament Interpreters Understand Jesus' Sayings and Parables, or the Sermon on the Mount?

New Testament interpreters distinguish the sayings of Jesus in the Synoptic Gospels from those in the Johannine tradition. In the Synoptics, the sayings-material is found in general to be of three sorts: isolated sayings, parables, and pronouncements (what R. Bultmann called apophthegms). The last-mentioned are sayings embedded in the narrative-tradition of the Synoptics, i.e., stories recounted for the sake of the pronouncement or punch-line enshrined in them. An example would be the story about showing Jesus the Roman denarius with Caesar's likeness on it and Jesus' consequent saying, "Render to Caesar . . ." (Mark 12:17), a narrative with dramatic details, which were preserved solely for the sake of the saying. Another example would be the story about the disciples plucking grain in the fields on the sabbath and Jesus' comment to the Pharisees that "the sabbath was made for man, not man for the sabbath" (Mark 2:27).

a. The isolated sayings seem to have floated around early Christian communities; they became detached from their historical contexts and eventually found themselves related to disparate material in different Gospels. An example of such sayings would be that about nothing being hidden except to be made manifest, which is derived by Luke (8:17) from the Marcan source (4:22), but which appears again in the Lucan Gospel in another form (12:2), parallel to Matt 10:26, and hence was derived from the "Q" source. As R. Bultmann has pointed out, these isolated sayings can be further subdivided into: (i) wisdom sayings; (ii) prophetic and apocalyptic sayings; (iii) legal sayings and Church rules; and (iv) "I"-sayings. Some of those in the third category reflect later Church problems and have been at least reformulated in terms of these problems, if they do indeed contain some authentic kernel.

b. Highly distinctive of the sayings-material in the Synoptic Gospels are the parables of Jesus. The Johannine tradition contains no *parabolai*, but on one occasion it passes on a *paroimia*, "a figurative saying" (10:6, referring to the preceding saying about the shepherd and the sheepfold [cf. John 16:25,29]). In most cases, the Synoptic parables are expanded similes, in which the story, though fictitious, is true to life (and specifically to life in first-century Palestine, with much Semitic coloring). This story teaches a truth (about the kingdom, about God's mercy, about the conduct of disciples) by illustration, but also by introducing a novel or strange twist which teases the hearer to further reflection or consideration. Most parables have only one point of comparison, but a few of them have an allegorizing tendency which identifies various figures or elements in the parable (e.g., the parable of the wicked vineyard-tenants, Mark 12:1–2 and par.). The parables are a didactic device, intended to disclose an obvious aspect of the kingdom, God, or conduct, but they are often quite subtle. This subtlety often elicited later "interpretations" of the parables, which have at times even been put on the lips of Jesus himself by the evangelists or by the traditions that they used. Take, for instance, the parable of the sower in Mark 4:3–20. The parable is given in vv. 3–8; v. 9 contains an isolated saying. Verses 10–13 are the early Church's explanation about why Jesus used parables, and vv. 14–20 the early Church's interpretation of the parable itself. Another example might be the parable of the dishonest manager in Luke 16:1–13. The parable itself is found in vv. 1–8a, but vv. 8b–9,10–12,13 supply three allegorical interpretations of the parable, i.e., three different homiletic applications which allegorize details in the story of vv. 1–8a, beyond the real point that the parable was intended to make. See further J. Jeremias, *The Parables of Jesus: Revised Edition* (New York: Scribner, 1963); R. E. Brown, *The Parables of the Gospels* (Glen Rock, N.J.: Paulist, 1963; my *Essays on the Semitic Background of the New Testament,* 161–84.

c. As interpreters seek to understand the sayings, parables, and pronouncements of the Synoptic tradition, they are not interested solely in stripping off the editorial accretions in order to recover the original *logia* or sayings and parables of Jesus. They also seek to understand the Gospel-context in which the sayings are now enshrined as well as what these might mean to a modern reader. Often enough, the redactional work of the evangelist has a theological thrust or an interpretive nuance which may be as important for Christians of our generation as the original sayings of Jesus themselves. Take, for example, the Lucan addition of "the Holy Spirit" to Jesus' saying about prayer being answered: "If you then who are evil know how to give good gifts to your own children, how much more will the Father from heaven give the Holy Spirit to those who ask him" (Luke 11:13). Contrast the more original "Q" form of the saying in Matt 7:11 and recall the Lucan emphasis on the role of the Spirit in Christian life. Some readers may be reluctant to admit this sort of "tampering" with the words of Jesus—even by an evangelist under inspiration. Seemingly, they might prefer to think that perhaps Jesus uttered the saying in a variant way on a different occasion. That solution is, of course, always theoretically *possible.* But given the complexity and frequency of the phenomenon, that solution is simply unsatisfactory.

d. In turning to the Johannine sayings, one encounters sayings that are independent of the Synoptics and derived from a tradition which makes Jesus speak quite differently. Bultmann once distinguished three sources of the Johannine Gospel: (i) a signs-source (the narratives of Jesus' miracles); (ii) the revelatory-discourse source; and (iii) the passion and resurrection stories. The Johannine sayings of Jesus would have been derived from the revelatory-discourse source. But there are many difficulties with that analysis, and his source-theory of the Johannine Gospel is widely questioned today.

The distinction that he made at least alerts the reader to the variety of material which is found in the Fourth Gospel. Rather than being derived from an earlier written source, the speeches are the composition of an author (and an editor [at least one]) who has structured the dialogues and narratives to his own purpose(s). The speeches are often repetitious and probably reflect different forms of the same discourse which have been incorporated into the Gospel. They are not, however, fabrications out of whole cloth. What may be historical in them has been overlaid with much else (especially with interpretive meditation).

The diversity of the Johannine speeches from the sayings-material in the Synoptics is not merely a matter of language in the sense of style or grammar, but rather in the realm of concepts and images. The Johannine speeches are characterized by a dualism of light and darkness, truth and falsehood, above and below; by a contrast of father and son; by numerous "I am" sayings, which differ from the "I"-sayings of the Synoptics (by the absolute use of "I am" or the use of it with symbolic predicates); and by highly distinctive images for salvation (water of life, bread of life, light of the world, gate of the sheepfold, etc.). What the speeches manifest in the long run is an understanding of Jesus, with a "high" christology, for which the Synoptics showed little interest. Though "the discourses consist of traditional sayings and explanatory developments" (R. E. Brown), there is certainly more of the latter than of the former. For an interpretation of the early Church context in which the Johannine Gospel came into being, see R. E. Brown, *The Community of the Beloved Disciple* (New York: Paulist, 1979).

e. As for the Sermon on the Mount (Matt 5:1–7:27), we recognize today that Matthew has here preserved for us a significant body of Jesus' sayings. Its ninety-nine verses stand in contrast, however, to the thirty verses of its Lucan parallel, the Sermon on the Plain (6:20–49). Both preserve the recollection of a significant, prolonged discourse that Jesus delivered toward the beginning of his Galilean ministry. (The Marcan sermon in parables, 4:1–33, may reflect the same recollection.) The Lucan and Matthean sermons are related: they have the same basic theme (the uprightness demanded of disciples by the kingship of God), the same exordium (beatitudes, though differing in number), the same conclusion (the parable of the two houses), and the same generic setting (reference to a mountain [Matt 5:1; Luke 6:12,17], and to the beginning of the ministry). They are both followed by the cure of a centurion's servant (Matt 8:5–13; Luke 7:1–10). The longer Matthean form of the sermon is explained in two ways: (i) Luke has omitted much material which would have meaning only in a specifically Jewish-Christian setting (e.g., what corresponds to Matt 5:17,19–20,21–24,27–28,33–39a,43; 6:1–8,16–18; 7:6,15); and (ii) Matthew has introduced many sayings which Luke uses elsewhere, e.g., to expand his travel account (Luke 9:51–18:14). This difference of treatment illustrates how these two evangelists have made use of the "Q" material, by inserting isolated sayings and parables into parts of their Gospels that they deemed important. The structure of the Matthean Sermon on the Mount is carefully worked out: (a) exordium (5:3–16, beatitudes, etc.); (b) thesis (5:17–20, esp. v. 20, which gives structure to the rest of the Sermon); (c) the uprightness of the scribes (5:21–48, six legal antitheses); (d) the uprightness of the Pharisees (6:1–18, sayings about three practices of Pharisaic piety: almsgiving, prayer, fasting); and (e) the uprightness of Jesus' disciples (6:19–7:27, a series of isolated sayings strung together, describing the transformation of human life demanded by God's new form of kingship). Many of the sayings in the Sermon on the Mount are to be traced back to Jesus himself; but some have clear Matthean formulation, e.g., the exceptive phrase in the prohibition of divorce (5:32; cf. 19:9), which is found only in Matthew. (One may contrast the earliest form of the prohibition in 1 Cor 7:10–11; the most primitive form in Luke 16:18; and the adapted form in Mark 10:11–12—all of them, however, absolute in their formulation, i.e., without an exception.—See further my article, "The Matthean Divorce Texts and Some New Palestinian Evidence," *TS* 37 [1976] 197–226; reprinted in *To Advance the Gospel: New Testament Studies*

[New York: Crossroad, 1981] 79–111.) Similarly Matthean is the formulation, "Our Father in heaven" in 6:9 (compare 5:16,45,48; 6:1,14 with Luke 11:2). In all, the Sermon is neither a perfectionist's code, nor an interim ethic, nor an exposé of the impossible ideal, nor a utopian dream, nor a new Torah. It represents rather the Matthean Jesus' radical demands for the transformation of human life.

7. How Do Contemporary New Testament Interpreters Understand the Miracle Stories?

Once again, we must distinguish the Synoptic and Johannine traditions about Jesus' miracles. In the Synoptic tradition four different types of miracle stories are recorded: (i) healings (possibly fifteen of them); (ii) exorcisms (five); (iii) resuscitations (two); and (iv) nature miracles (six, with one of them a "would be" [Matt 17:24–27, the story about the coin in the fish's mouth, the outcome of which we never learn]). In the Johannine tradition, seven miracles are recounted in the so-called Book of Signs (chaps. 1–12) and another in the appendix (chap. 21). Of these, three are healings, one a resuscitation, and four are nature miracles. Among the latter, two have parallels in the Synoptics: the feeding of five thousand (6:1–13; cf. Mark 6:30–44) and Jesus' walking on the water (6:16–21; cf. Mark 6:45–52).

a. What is significant here is the independent multiple attestation of a tradition about Jesus' performance of miraculous deeds. They form part of a tradition which considered them no less important than the words of Jesus.

b. Further significance is seen in the terms used for these deeds, since they are never called "miracles" (a word derived from a later Latin theological tradition, *miraculum,* and predicated of them—often with anachronistic nuances). In the Synoptics they are usually called *dynameis,* "deeds of might" (or "power"), Mark 6:2,5; Luke 10:13; 19:37; Matt 13:54. In John they are rather referred to as *erga,* "works" (e.g., 5:36; 10:25,32) or even *sēmeia,* "signs" (e.g., 2:11;

4:54; 9:16). The latter term immediately shifts our attention from them as deeds that might transcend what has been called the laws of nature to their religious value and significance, which is invariably found in the Gospel-stories that recount them. The former term, *dynameis,* suggests rather something about the person of Jesus and the kingdom that he announces. There is, thus, a christological aspect to them. Luke, however, has associated an added apologetic nuance with them, when he writes in Acts 2:22 about Jesus of Nazareth, "a man (*andra*) attested to you by God with mighty works, wonders, and signs." Yet not even Luke presses on to the conclusion that is so often drawn from this way of considering them, viz., to the divinity of Jesus, or at least to the plausibility of believing in it (as in traditional apologetics). For Luke, Jesus is rather God's attested agent, later described in the same speech of Peter, indeed, as "Lord and Christ" (2:36). In the other Synoptics, however, the miracles of Jesus serve much more to announce that the kingship of God is now breaking anew into human history and into that of Palestinian Judaism in particular. They are the concrete evidence that a new understanding of God's kingship is authentic.

c. For modern readers the miracle stories of the Gospels raise the problem of credibility. In this connection we should recall the following. *First,* some of the stories have acquired folkloric accretions. An indication of this is given in the most fantastic of the miracle stories, that of the Gerasene demoniac and the swine (Mark 5:1–20). The trace of such accretion is present in the ending, "And he went away and began to tell in all the Decapolis how much Jesus had done for him. . . ." Moreover, the accounts of this miracle defy all attempts to locate the scene historically near a sea (Mark 5:13, which Luke corrects to "the lake" [8:33]). The manuscript tradition gives three sites for it, two of which are far from Lake Tiberias: *Gerasa* (= modern Jerash, about thirty miles to the southeast) and *Gadara* (about six miles to the southeast). A third site, *Gergesa,* supposedly on the eastern edge of the lake, is poorly attested; this name is often traced to Origen, but probably comes from an earlier tradition, which may have been invented precisely to solve the problem of location. Even if one were to admit with Johannes Weiss that the paroxysm accompanying the exorcism set the herd of swine in motion, they would have become the most energetic hogs in history to reach such a cliff. The story is of the sort that one finds in the apocryphal gospel tradition of the infancy of Jesus; it represents a certain climax of the miraculous tradition, which has invaded even the New Testament writings themselves. By contrast, most of the other miracle stories are told with a sobriety which has often been called striking.

Second, in several accounts of healings or exorcisms one finds clear instances of protological thinking. Persons afflicted with what we would call today mental disturbances were regarded as possessed because observers were unable to analyze properly the causes of the maladies in question, and consequently ascribed them to a demon. Mark 9:14–29 tells of the exorcism of a boy whose father said that he had a "dumb spirit"; in the Matthean parallel (17:15) he is described as "moonstruck" (*selēniazetai*). Anyone reading that story today recognizes the boy to be epileptic. Here we are dealing with what has been called "demon-sickness" (or "demon-disasters"). A demon is invoked to explain the cause of the sickness or disaster. Jesus is said to "rebuke" the fever of Simon's mother-in-law (Luke 4:39; but cf. Mark 1:31; Matt 8:15), i.e., he is regarded as having rebuked the spirit protologically considered to be causing the high fever. Similarly, he "rebukes" the winds and the waves (Mark 4:39 and par.), i.e., he is regarded as having rebuked the demon or spirit causing the squall. Undoubtedly, Jesus shared some of the protological thinking himself, being a child of his time.

Third, having thus demythologized some of the fantasy and the protological thinking found in some of the miracle stories, we are left with a still more basic problem. For if, in reality, Jesus did not exorcise a demon, but cured a mentally-ill person, was it less of a miracle? Some New Testament interpreters have sought to write off the entire tradition of Jesus' miracles in the New Testament by ascribing them to the Hellenistic background of the Gospels and the concern of early Christians to depict Jesus as another *theios anēr,* "divine man," or thaumaturge of the Greco-Roman world. True, one can find at times parallels in contemporary literature to some of the miracle stories in the Gospels (even with a close resemblance in form). But the extent to which the miracle stories, as we have them, are to be wholly attributed to Hellenistic Christianity is precisely the difficulty. The *Genesis Apocryphon* of Qumran Cave 1 knows of a tradition about Abram's curing the Pharaoh Zoan of an affliction caused by an evil spirit sent because the Pharaoh had carried off Sarai, Abram's wife; this he did by laying on his hands and praying for the Pharaoh (20:29; cf. Luke 4:40–41). This example reveals that miraculous cures were as much at home in Palestinian Jewish literature as in the larger Greco-Roman world. And the historian Josephus, a Palestinian Jew, had no difficulty in accepting the miraculous in Old Testament accounts because they were for him manifestations of God's "providence" (*pronoia*) and "power" (*dynamis*); see *Ant.* 2.16,1 §336.

On the other hand, Paul's letters show no interest in the miraculous activity of Jesus, even though he did not fail to speak of such in his own experience and life (see 2 Cor 12:12; cf. 1 Cor 12:10,28,29; Gal 3:5). But then, how little interest does Paul show in anything in the earthly career of Jesus prior to the Last Supper! Luke's references to Jesus' miracles in Acts (2:22; 10:38) do not represent an independent testimony about them; they are clearly dependent on his own Gospel.

Fourth, several other aspects of the miracle stories of the Gospels have to be considered. (a) Whether the devil, the Pharisees, Herod, or just ordinary people sought "signs" or miracles from Jesus as evidence that he was sent by God, the New Testament writers attest that he refused to perform them either in his own interest or to satisfy the curiosity of his contemporaries (see Mark 6:5a; 8:11–13; 15:31–32; Matt 4:5–7; Luke 4:9–12; 23:8–9). (b) The Gospels never depict Jesus miraculously punishing human beings, as Peter does to Ananias and Sapphira (Acts 5:1–11), or Paul to Elymas the magician (Acts 13:10–11), or the angel to Zechariah (Luke 1:20)—all, significantly enough, in Luke-Acts. In cursing the barren fig tree, Jesus is portrayed using his power on a non-human creature—in an act symbolic of the fate of Jerusalem's house of prayer (see Mark 11:12–25; cf. Matt 21:18–22—significantly omitted by Luke). (c) One has to recognize the symbolic value and meaning of the miracles of Jesus which are recounted. I do not refer to the specific symbolism associated with one or other miracle (e.g., the way that the evangelists have—with hindsight—made the accounts of the multiplication of the loaves foreshadow the Eucharist). I mean rather the symbolism of the conquering of evil; the miracles thus announce a new form of God's regal activity in the conquest of evil afflicting his people. Sin, physical or mental illness, disasters in nature, even death itself, are forms of the power of evil in human life. Jesus is depicted possessing the power of the kingdom, which clearly makes known that a counterforce is present among human beings to cope with such evil. (d) An element that is so frequently associated with the miracles of Jesus in both the Synoptics and John is faith—not a belief in demons, but rather faith in the salvific power which is now manifest in Jesus, the agent of Yahweh. In such Gospel stories it is not yet (in Stage I) full *Christian* faith. Such faith would presuppose the resurrection of Jesus. It is rather an awareness of and trust in God's providence manifest in Jesus.

d. In the long run, the greatest difficulty sensed today with the Gospel miracles is a philosophic one: Can God or does God intervene in human history by such extraordinary means? This is a philosophic problem born of an outlook which stems from the *Aufklärung* or Enlightenment. To try to solve that problem, using examples drawn from ancient texts or the early Christian heritage, is misguided. The Gospel accounts, of which the miracle stories form part of the warp and woof, were not composed to answer such a problem.

8. How Are the Gospel Accounts of Jesus' Baptism To Be Understood?

References to Jesus' baptism are found in all four Gospels (Mark 1:9–11; Matt 3:13–17; Luke 3:21–22; John 1:30–34) and indirectly in Acts (10:37–38). There is no reason to question the historicity of the fact that Jesus of Nazareth, toward the beginning of his own ministry, submitted himself to a ritual washing performed by John the Baptist. The indirect reference to the baptism in the speech of Peter in Acts 10 may simply reflect Luke's own account in 3:21–22. However, some have thought that Peter's speech at the conversion of Cornelius contains a brief summary of early Christian kerygmatic preaching (see C. H. Dodd, *The Apostolic Preaching and Its Developments* [London: Hodder and Stoughton, 1936] 47–48). If that theory has any validity, then the reference may be even earlier than that in Mark 1:9–11.

a. John's baptizing is attested extra-biblically. Josephus (*Ant.* 18.5,2 §116–17) refers to him as one "called the Baptist," knows of his *baptismos,* and speaks of it in connection with a pardon of sins. Moreover, John's baptism can be plausibly viewed against the background of the ritual washings in the contemporary Palestinian Jewish Qumran community, which practiced (daily) lustrations in a belief that they symbolized God's refinement (by fire) of the human frame and a purification of it by "a spirit of holiness" (*Manual of Discipline* [1QS] 4:20–22). The Synoptic Gospels have related John's baptism to his preaching of repentance for the forgiveness of sins (Mark 1:4,5; Matt 3:6,11; Luke 3:3).

b. There are differences of detail in the Gospel accounts of the baptism of Jesus. Whereas all four evangelists relate the incident to the River Jordan, they do so with slight differences (see Mark 1:9; Matt 3:13; Luke 3:3; 4:1; John 1:28; 3:26 ["beyond the Jordan"]). The differences in other details are more pronounced. In Mark 1:9; Matt 3:13–16 Jesus is explicitly baptized by John, whereas in Luke

3:21–22 no agent is named, "When . . . Jesus too was baptized." The reason for Luke's silence is that he has already recounted the imprisonment of the Baptist in vv. 19–20; he thus finishes off this story of John before he begins that of Jesus, and hence he cannot—in the logic of his own narrative-sequence—mention the baptism by John. Note that in John 1:24–34 too it is never said that John baptized Jesus or even that Jesus was baptized; this is *implicit,* however, in the words addressed to John by him who sent him to baptize. In this difference one detects the interests of the evangelist taking precedence over mere detail.

In Mark 1:10, after the baptism, we are told that Jesus "saw the heavens opened and the Spirit descending on him"—an experience of Jesus himself. In Luke 3:21–22 Jesus, having been baptized, was at prayer, when "the heavens happened to open and the Holy Spirit descended in bodily form like a dove upon him." Here the evangelist has, as he often does elsewhere (5:16; 6:12; 9:18; 11:2; 22:32,41; 23:46), depicted Jesus at prayer at a crucial moment of his career. But, more importantly, the opening of the heavens and the descent of the Spirit are recounted as perceptible to others. In Matt 3:16 Jesus "saw the Spirit of God descending on him" (as in Mark 1:10), but the opening of the heavens is narrated as publicly perceptible ("Behold, the heavens were opened"). In John 1:32–33 the Baptist is the only one who saw "the Spirit descend as a dove from heaven." Hence the narratives differ as to whether Jesus or others or the Baptist perceived what was happening.

Moreover, in Mark 1:11 and Luke 3:22 the heavenly voice addresses Jesus himself, "You are my beloved Son; in you I have taken delight." But in Matt 3:17 the heavenly voice publicly declares, "This is my beloved Son. . . ." In John 1:33 no voice from heaven is heard at the baptism or says anything about Jesus' sonship; but the one who has sent John to baptize has already told *him,* "As for the one on whom *you see* the Spirit descend and remain, he it is who baptizes with the Holy Spirit."

c. From such differences of detail it is clear that we can no longer reconstruct exactly what happened at Jesus' baptism itself (in Stage I of the Gospel tradition)—beyond a generic realization that early Christians associated with Jesus' baptism by John a heavenly intervention making known his elect status. But it is no longer clear how this happened or to whom the declaration was made (to Jesus? to the bystanders? to John?). This should instruct us that the importance of the scene in the Gospel tradition lay in something else.

d. In the earliest Gospel the baptism scene (vv. 9–11) serves to identify Jesus of Nazareth for the readers: he is heaven's chosen agent for the preaching of "God's Gospel" (1:14), now identified as "beloved Son" (with a possible allusion to the servant-theme of Isa 42:1 [LXX]). This role he plays in the Marcan Gospel as he is subsequently depicted preaching, teaching, healing, and announcing the kingdom of God. This initial identification of Jesus is the real import of the Marcan baptism scene—all the more important because this Gospel lacks an infancy narrative and the use of christological titles associated with that part of the Gospel tradition. The real question is what the baptism scene reveals to the readers of the Matthean and Lucan Gospels which have already identified Jesus with diverse titles in the infancy narratives themselves. In the case of the Lucan Gospel, the infancy narrative was almost certainly prefixed at a later stage, after the composition of the bulk of the Gospel. Even though Jesus has already been identified as Son in 1:32,35, Luke has retained the baptism scene because it was associated with the traditional beginning of the story of Jesus' ministry and becomes important for him as the "beginning" (*archē*) of the period of Jesus in his conception of salvation history.

e. To what extent can we determine the nature of the personal experience of the historical Jesus on the occasion of his baptism at the beginning of his public ministry? This is difficult to say. Apart from the generic problem of the consciousness of the historical Jesus (see §2 above), the differences of detail in this episode compound the difficulty. Mark has clearly depicted the sequel to the baptism as a personal experience of Jesus, and Luke does so partly. But Matthew has made of the heavenly declaration a public proclamation, and John a heavenly revelation to the Baptist alone. Neither of the latter two Gospels hints at what Jesus himself might have experienced.

It is often said (in popular treatments) that the baptism of Jesus was the occasion when he became aware that he was God's messiah. This, however, is an oversimplification. *First of all,* the wording of the heavenly declaration in the Synoptics does not identify Jesus as an anointed agent, a messiah. It speaks in terms of his sonship and possibly of his servanthood. *Second,* Ps 2:7 ("You are my son; this day I have begotten you"), which is often introduced to support this interpretation, is found only in a few manuscripts, but not in the best of them, in the Lucan Gospel tradition. Moreover, one would have to show that this royal psalm was actually understood as messianic (as referring to an *expected* messiah to sit on David's throne) in contemporary Palestinian Judaism—which cannot be shown. *Third,* only Luke among New Testament writers interprets Jesus' baptism as his anointing with the Holy Spirit (Acts 10:38). To extrapolate from such a later Christian theologoumenon to the consciousness of the historical Jesus of Nazareth is very problematic.

f. A final comment has to be made about the conversation between John the Baptist and Jesus in Matt 3:14–15 (John would have prevented Jesus from being baptized by him, saying, "I ought to be baptized by you, and are you coming to me?" Jesus answered, "Let it be so now. It is fitting for us to fulfill all righteousness in this way"). The conversation, recorded only in Matthew, gives a distinctive Matthean coloring to the baptism scene (as did the Lucan addition about Jesus at prayer); it would have to be related to the evangelist's larger theme of righteousness (cf., e.g., 21:32). Two remarks should be added: (1) The "fulfillment of all righteousness" stresses the relationship of John's ministry and baptism to God's salvific will; the Matthean Jesus, in submitting to John's baptism, acknowledges the Baptist's role and the heavenly origin of the salvific way of righteousness which his preaching announced among his contemporaries. "Let it be so now." (2) Jesus' submission to the Baptist's washing as a sign of repentance for the remission of sins implies at least his identification of himself with sinful humanity seeking a way of righteousness given by God through John. Whether it was meant to express an awareness of sin on the part of Jesus himself is another matter. This touches again on the consciousness problem discussed above, and it may be asked whether the Matthean episode was meant to answer such a problem. John's protest may reflect much more the awareness of the early Church which otherwise insisted on the sinlessness of Christ Jesus (see 2 Cor 5:21; John 8:46; Heb 4:15; 7:26) and the forerunner-relation of John's baptism to early Christian baptism.

9. How Do Modern Interpreters of the New Testament Understand Jesus' Words to Peter at Caesarea Philippi?

The question is concerned with the scene of Peter's confessing of Jesus' messiahship in the Synoptic tradition (Mark 8:27–33; Matt 16:13 23; Luke 9:18–22). Only Mark and Matthew mention the localization of the episode at Caesarea Philippi. Luke omits all reference to locale, only placing the episode toward the end of Jesus' Galilean ministry, shortly before he begins his journey to Jerusalem (9:51). It is, in fact, the first episode with which Luke resumes his use of Marcan material after the so-called big omission of this material in his Gospel (= Mark 6:45–8:26). Since it was outside of Galilee, Luke would not want to admit that Jesus was at Caesarea Philippi. Given the literary build-up of his Gospel in which Jesus moves resolutely from his Galilean ministry to Jerusalem, the city of destiny, an episode situated at Caesarea Philippi would prove to be an added distraction.

a. Many commentators regard John 6:67–71 as a related form of the same tradition. The episode there is located in the synagogue of Capernaum, again in Galilee (6:59), and Peter acknowledges Jesus to be not Messiah, but "Lord" and the "Holy One of God." Given its general relation to the Galilean ministry, there may be some connection between this Johannine confession of Peter and the Synoptic form as found in Mark.

b. In the Synoptic form Jesus asks his disciples, "Who do people say I am?" Having received various answers (John the Baptist, Elijah, one of the prophets [Matthew adds, "Jeremiah"], Jesus then asks the disciples, "Who do you say I am?" Peter speaks up. In Mark 8:29 he acknowledges Jesus to be "the Messiah" (*or* "Christ," *ho christos*); in Luke 9:20, as "God's Messiah" (*or* "the Christ of God"); in Matthew 16:16, as "the Messiah (*or* Christ), the Son of the living God." The tradition about his confession has obviously grown.

c. In Mark (8:30) and Luke (9:21) Jesus immediately charges the disciples to tell this to no one and proceeds to make the first announcement of his passion, death, and resurrection (as the Son of Man). Though Luke omits it, Mark adds Peter's uncomprehending protest, to which Jesus replies with an epithet for Peter and a rebuke: Peter is identified as Satan and "not on the side of God but of human beings."

d. In the oldest form of the tradition about Peter's confession (Mark 8:27–33), there is thus an acknowledgement by Peter, the spokesman for the disciples, that Jesus is the Messiah. The fact that Jesus forbids the disciples to repeat that acknowledgement and that he counters it with a corrective saying about his own fate reveals that he did not accept the implications of the title as used by Peter. The extent to which Peter (and other disciples) would have considered Jesus to be a messiah in a political sense is difficult for us to ascertain today. Certainly Peter's acknowledgement of Jesus as Messiah cannot be understood in Stage I of the Gospel tradition with all the connotations of the title in Stages II or III (see §3 above). Peter's confession would have to be taken as an indication of a breakthrough of some sort in the disciples' awareness about who Jesus was, though only in an inceptive way. But that title in no way implies an allegiance to Jesus which would keep Peter from eventually denying him (14:66–72) or the disciples from deserting him (14:50–52). For the connotation, see further §18 below.

e. As used in the Marcan Gospel, Peter's confession and Jesus' subsequent sayings form a turning point in the literary structure of that writing. Up to this point (inclusive) Jesus imposes silence on those who would use titles of him; after that point the use of titles changes, and the climax of the revelation about him in the Marcan Gospel is reached when a pagan Roman centurion declares about the crucified Jesus, "Surely, this man was the Son of God" (15:39).

f. The Lucan reuse of Marcan material is significant for three things: (1) The title is slightly expanded: Jesus is "God's Messiah" (9:20). However, this is not radically different from the Marcan confession. (2) Luke omits all reference to Peter's protest and Jesus' rebuke. This fits in with the general tendency in the Lucan writings, in which the disciples are not portrayed as deserting Jesus. (In fact, even at the crucifixion among those standing not far off from Jesus are not only the women who had followed him from Galilee, but "all his acquaintances" (*hoi gnōstoi,* masculine! [23:49], so that his disciples have not deserted him.) Peter will, indeed, deny Jesus in the Lucan Gospel; but Jesus will pray for him (22:32), and he will be converted. (3) The confession of Peter plays a different role in the Lucan Gospel, not enhancing Peter so much, as it does in Matthew, but supplying an important christological assertion. Because of the big omission (see above), Peter's confession comes in Luke's sequence on the heels of Herod's crucial question, "Who is this about whom I hear such talk?" (9:9). It thus proves to be one of several christological answers given to that question in chapter 9, which is a peculiarly Lucan refashioning of the Synoptic tradition. (See further my commentary, *The Gospel according to Luke I-IX* [AB 28; Garden City, N.Y.: Doubleday, 1981] 756–58.)

g. Matthew too has made use of the Marcan story; its parallel is found in 16:13–16a,20–23 (with Peter's protest and Jesus' rebuke retained). But the Matthean Gospel has in this instance some additional material (vv. 16b–19), which further expands (significantly) Peter's confession: Jesus is not only "the Messiah," but "the Son of the living God." To this acknowledgement Jesus now replies with a recognition that Peter's insight has been granted by God ("Flesh and blood have not revealed this to you, but my Father who is in heaven"). Jesus then bestows on Simon a title, *Petros* (masculine), "Rock," and promises to build his Church unshakably on "this rock" (*petra*, feminine) and give him authority in it. Having pronounced a beatitude over Simon Peter and promised him a significant role or function, Jesus charges his disciples to tell no one that he is the Messiah (16:20)—thus resuming the Marcan form of the story with Peter's protest and Jesus' rebuke. In the present Matthean context the retention of this material clashes with the beatitudes and the promises.

Verses 16b–19 are an addition to the story inherited from Mark, added by the evangelist who is using material from another part of the Gospel tradition. In John 21:15–17 the risen Christ, having appeared to seven disciples in Galilee at Lake Tiberias, confers authority on Simon Peter as he commissions Peter (three times over) to feed his sheep. Whereas former generations of interpreters often distinguished the *promise* of a Petrine function to Simon (in Matthew 16) and the *conferral* of it (in John 21), the modern tendency is to regard the additional material in Matt 16:16b–19 merely as a variant in the Synoptic Gospel tradition of that in the Johannine scene. Matthew would then have retrojected an episode from the tradition about appearances of the risen Christ into the public ministry itself. The acknowledgement of Jesus as "the Son of the living God" is certainly more plausible on the lips of Peter after his denial and the experience of the resurrection than it is at Caesarea Philippi. Such a christological title as "Son of the living God" could readily have been joined to another one, "the Messiah," more suited to the ministry itself, thus producing in Matt 16:16 a double confession on the lips of Peter. This post-resurrection matrix for the material in vv. 16b–19 also provides a plausible setting for the beatitude pronounced over Peter by Jesus and for the Church-founding promises made to him, a setting far more plausible than in the ministry itself.

h. This theory would also provide a plausible explanation for what has always been a major problem in the episode of Peter's confession: If Jesus had said all this (vv. 17–19) to Simon at Caesarea Philippi, how could Mark (and Luke) have failed to find any trace of these words in the tradition about the Galilean ministry? If Matt 16:13–19 were the more correct record of what had happened at Caesarea Philippi, how could the tradition have arisen in such a truncated form as that now found in Mark 8 and Luke 9? It seems rather likely that Matthew has followed his custom of adding things—in this case, to the sayings of both Simon Peter and Jesus.

i. Lastly, this theory also explains why the word "Church" (*ekklēsia*) appears only in the Matthean form of the episode, and nowhere else in the Gospel tradition (save, again, in a Matthean passage, 18:17). Neither Mark, nor Luke (in his Gospel), nor John ever portrays Jesus speaking of his community of followers as "the Church." Even in Acts it is only with the beginning of the story of Saul/Paul that it begins to appear regularly (8:1 and thereafter). (Before that it does appear in Acts 5:11, in *Luke's own* comment about fear falling on the "whole Church" as a result of the Ananias and Sapphira affair—where Luke uses it as a term borrowed from the common usage of his own day to describe a condition in the earlier community [see my *Pauline Theology: A Brief Sketch* (Englewood Cliffs, N.J.: Prentice-Hall, 1967) 75–76; *JBC,* art. 79, §149–50].) By contrast, the word "Church" is found abundantly in the (genuine and questionably genuine) Pauline letters. It was thus already part of the Christian tradition for some time prior to the composition of the Gospels, but it has not entered the Gospel tradition, save twice in Matthew. It seems that Matthew has incorporated into his Gospel a term for the early community which found vogue in the extra-evangelical tradition of early Christianity. This naturally leaves open to speculation the name that the historical Jesus might have used for this group of his followers during the ministry, if any.

j. In the Matthean Gospel the expanded episode (16:13–23) joins two others in which material has been added by the evangelist and all of which enhance the Petrine role: Matt 14:22–33 (Peter's walking on the waters, to be compared with Mark 6:45–52 [omitted by Luke] and Matt 17:24–27 (the finding of a coin in the fish's mouth, an episode exclusive to Matthew). All three episodes relate Peter closely to Jesus. They describe the Petrine function in a manner which is unique to this Gospel. It has, in turn, had a marked emphasis on the developing ecclesiology of the early Church beyond that of any other Gospel. See further R. E. Brown et al. (eds.), *Peter in the New Testament* (New York: Paulist; Minneapolis: Augsburg, 1973) 75–107.

10. How Are Jesus' Words and Actions at the Last Supper To Be Understood?

The question refers to the passages in 1 Cor 11:23–25; Mark 14:17–25; Matt 26:20–29; Luke 22:14–38; John 13:1–17:26, even though the name "Last Supper" is never found in any of them. That is a development out of the reference to Jesus' "dining" (1 Cor 11:25), which two verses earlier is dated to "the night on which he was betrayed." Cf. John 13:1–2 for another way of phrasing it. The nature of that meal which Jesus took with his disciples shortly before his arrest and death is, however, variously described in the New Testament.

a. The Johannine Gospel restricts Jesus' actions at that meal to the washing of the feet of the disciples (apart from his giving a dipped morsel of food to Judas, 13:26). The washing of the feet was a symbolic act not understood at the time by those present, but intended by the evangelist as an "example" to portray Jesus' fundamental attitude of lowly service to those whom the Father had given him (his chosen followers): "that you too should do as I have done to you" (13:15). This act, unrecorded in the earlier tradition about this supper, either Pauline or Synoptic, is evidently intended to give a symbolic summation of the whole life of Jesus.

The Johannine account likewise depicts Jesus uttering several lengthy discourses (14:1–16:33 [composite]; 17:1–26). These are again unknown to Paul and the Synoptics (Luke 22:21–38 includes four sayings of Jesus in his account, quite different in content, however, from the lengthy discourses of the Johannine Jesus). This Johannine tradition about Jesus' words at the "Last Supper" (interpreting his mission, his relation to the Father, the coming of the Spirit-Paraclete, and the mission of the disciples) obviously developed independently of the other early traditions about that meal.

b. The earliest reference in the New Testament to the "Last Supper" (and what soon grew out of it) is found in 1 Corinthians (written about A.D. 56), where Paul, even before he recounts what Jesus did and said at it, speaks of a participation of Christians in "the table of the Lord" (10:21). He thus refers to what was already a well-established ritual custom among Corinthian Christians. At it they shared in a "cup of blessing" (10:16a), which Paul now interprets as "a participation in the blood of Christ" (v. 16b) and in a "breaking of bread" (v. 16c), which is "a participation in the body of Christ" (v. 16d): "All partake of the one bread" (10:17). Here Paul alludes to a Christian rite, which he even compares with "sacrifices" of "the people of Israel" (10:18) and other sacrifices of "pagans" (10:20), as he emphasizes the idea of partnership or participation of those involved in it.

To what rite Paul alludes becomes clear when he refers to it as "the Lord's supper" (11:20) and shortly thereafter recounts its origin in actions and words of Jesus at a supper taken before his arrest. In 11:23–25 he thus records the earliest account of the institution of that rite: How on the night of his betrayal, Jesus took bread, gave thanks (to God), broke it, and said, "This is my body, which is for you," adding the directive to re-enact this action in memory of him. Similarly, "after supper," he took a cup of wine, said of it, "This cup is the new covenant in my blood," and repeated the directive. This tradition Paul inherited and passed on (1 Cor 11:23a).

c. Independently, the Synoptic evangelists were heirs to a similar "Last Supper" tradition (Mark 14:22–25; Matt 26:26–29; Luke 22:17–20). These passages belong to a larger context in which disciples are sent by Jesus to make preparations for the celebration of the Passover at the beginning of the "first day of Unleavened Bread" (Mark 14:12; Matt 26:17; Luke 22:7). In these accounts the Matthean closely follows the Marcan, whereas the Lucan is tributary to a separate tradition, which is in some respects similar to the Pauline (e.g., the reference to the cup "after supper" [22:20] and the inclusion of the memento-directive [22:19c]). But in others the Lucan account is quite independent too of the Pauline (e.g., the mention of two cups [22:17,20]; the relation of the eating of the Passover[-lamb] to Jesus' own suffering [22:15]). (N.B. Recent Greek manuscript-discoveries make it clear that vv. 19bc–20 were really part of the genuine Lucan text; so they are to be retained in translations and not relegated to footnotes, as has been done at times in this century by those translators who have followed a fad once started by Westcott and Hort in 1881 [see Nestle–Aland[26]].)

d. A classic problem must now be mentioned. In the Johannine Gospel Jesus eats the "Last Supper" with his disciples at sundown at the beginning of the Parasceve (the preparation day *before* the Passover itself, 18:28b). But in the Synoptics it is eaten at sundown as the Passover begins (Mark 14:16c; Matt 26:19b; Luke 22:13c) or at the beginning of the "(first) day of Unleavened Bread." Was the "Last Supper" a Passover-meal or not? According to all four evangelists the meal would have taken place on what we call Thursday evening. But was the Thursday-night/Friday a Passover (as the Synoptics suggest) or a Parasceve (as the Johannine tradition suggests)? Which tradition, then, is correct, the Synoptic or the Johannine? It is difficult to say. Attempts to explain the difference of the day in the two traditions by appealing to the use of different calendars, Essene and Pharisaic (or temple), only raise more problems than they solve. It might be worth recalling that the baraita of the Babylonian Talmud (*Sanhedrin 43*a [referred to in §2 above]) mentions that Yeshu was "hanged on the eve of Passover."

Early Christian theology may have dictated the preferences of those who fashioned the differing pre-Gospel traditions which were used by the evangelists. We can only speculate about such preferences. The Synoptic tradition may have preferred to portray Jesus eating the "Last Supper" with his disciples as an interpretive replacement of the Passover-meal of old (this preference emerges most clearly in Luke 22:15–16). On the other hand, the motif of Jesus as "the lamb of God" (John 1:36) may have contributed to the preference to depict his dying on the cross about the time on the Parasceve when the lambs were being slaughtered for the coming sundown-meal at the beginning of Passover. Hence even though the "Last Supper" would not have been eaten at the beginning of Passover in the Johannine tradition, an association of Jesus' *death* with the Passover-lamb may be suggested. Recall further the typical sense given to Num 9:12 (the prohibition to break a bone of the Passover-lamb) when it is used to explain why Jesus' legs were not broken, but his side pierced instead (John 19:33–36). Recall too the Pauline allusion to an ancient tradition which already regarded Christ as "our Passover (*or* Passover-lamb)" in 1 Cor 5:7.

In either case a strong early Christian tradition, reflected in the Pauline and Synoptic accounts, traced the celebration of the eucharistic liturgy to the words and actions of Jesus at the "Last Supper." Even the venerable name "Eucharist" for that liturgy is derived from a participle used in the Pauline and Synoptic accounts to describe one of Jesus' actions, *eucharistēsas,* "having given thanks" (1 Cor 11:24; Mark 14:23; Matt 26:27; Luke 22:17,19).

e. However, what has been thus preserved about Jesus' words and actions at the "Last Supper" in these varied traditions has been preserved with nuances, and with neither unanimity nor word-for-word exactitude. Whereas the Pauline and the Synoptic tradition clearly relates the Eucharist to that meal, the Johannine does not; and the traditions differ as to whether it was a Passover-meal or not. Moreover, the words of institution recorded in the Pauline and Synoptic accounts are not uniformly transmitted (see below). It is generally thought that the divergences reflect formulas already in use in different early liturgical settings, which were no longer primarily concerned with the *ipsissima verba Iesu,* but with the significance of Jesus' words and actions at the "Last Supper" for his followers and all humanity. The Marcan-Matthean formula possibly reflects a Jerusalemite usage, the Pauline-Lucan possibly an Antiochene. In any case, it is puzzling why more fidelity or unanimity would not have been displayed. One might have thought that the early Christians would have retained exactly at least this part of the Gospel tradition! Yet the situation itself offers a salutary corrective to our modern, twentieth-century preoccupations.

f. When we consider the words uttered by Jesus at the "Last Supper" over the bread and the cup of wine, we must note, *first of all,* the diversity of the tradition. Here are the various reports of Jesus' words over the bread *(arton)*:

1 Cor 11:24
"This is my body which is for you" (*RSV*).
Touto mou estin to sōma to hyper hymōn
[Note order of Greek words!]

Mark 14:22
"Take; this is my body" (*RSV*).
Labete, touto estin to sōma mou

Matt 26:26
"Take, eat; this is my body" (*RSV*).
Labete, phagete, touto estin to sōma mou

Luke 22:19
"This is my body, which is given for you" (*RSV*).
Touto estin to sōma mou to hyper hymōn didomenon

These words of Jesus over the bread may be reflected in the Johannine tradition about the bread of life:

John 6:51

"I am the living bread which came down from heaven; if any one eats of this bread, he will live forever; and the bread which I shall give for the life of the world is my flesh" (*RSV*).

Egō eimi ho artos ho zōn ho ek tou ouranou katabas. ean tis phagē ek toutou tou artou, zēsei eis ton aiōna. kai ho artos de hon egō dōsō hē sarx mou estin hyper tēs tou kosmou zōēs.

Here are the various reports of Jesus' words over the cup of wine:

1 Cor 11:25

"This cup is the new covenant in my blood" (*RSV*).

Touto to potērion hē kainē diathēkē estin en tō emō haimati

Mark 14:24

"This is my blood of the covenant, which is poured out for many" (*RSV*).

Touto estin to haima mou tēs diathēkēs to ekchynnomenon hyper pollōn

Matt 26:27–28

"Drink of it, all of you; for this is my blood of the covenant, which is poured out for many for the forgiveness of sins" (*RSV*).

Piete ex autou pantes, touto gar estin to haima mou tēs diathēkēs to peri pollōn ekchynnomenon eis aphesin hamartiōn

Luke 22:20
"This cup which is poured out for you is the new covenant
in my blood" (*RSV*). [Words over the second cup; cf.
22:17b]
*Touto to potērion hē kainē diathēkē estin en tō emō haimati
mou to hyper hymōn ekchynnomenon*

Confronted with such diversity, one may well ask, "Well, just what
formula did Jesus use on that historic occasion?" Who can say? And
the problem is compounded when one recalls that what we have is
almost certainly varying forms of a Greek translation of what he
probably uttered in Aramaic.

    Second, in these formulas there is an element that identifies Je-
sus' body and blood with the bread and wine and also an interpretive
element. One should learn to distinguish the two.

    f. The words uttered by Jesus over the bread and the cup of
wine in the Pauline and Synoptic accounts of the supper may be an
imitation of those uttered by the head of the Jewish family which ate
together the Passover-meal: "This is the bread of affliction which our
fathers had to eat as they came out of Egypt" (see J. Jeremias, *Eucharistic Words of Jesus* [Philadelphia: Fortress, 1977] 54–57; cf. G.
Dalman, *Jesus-Jeshua: Studies in the Gospels* [New York: Ktav,
1971] 139). Such an interpretive formula as the background for
"This is my body" or even "This is my blood of the covenant" would
supply a Passover-nuance to the words of institution. An objection,
however, has often been raised: The Synoptic (and Pauline) accounts
fail to mention the essentials of the Passover-meal (the lamb, the har-
oseth-sauce, etc.). This objection has its own problems, in that we are
not sure how *to pascha* in the New Testament is to be translated.
Should it be merely "the Passover" or "the Passover-lamb" (Mark
14:12,14,16; Matt 26:17,19; Luke 22:7,11,13,15)? Cf. Matt 26:23.
Such elements would support the Passover-connotation of the insti-
tuted Eucharist.

    g. The eucharistic words of Jesus have an element of ambiguity.

Does the Greek verb *estin* in these formulas mean "is really" (as the verb "to be" denotes in Matt 3:17; 10:2; 13:55; 14:2) or "is symbolically/spiritually" (as in John 10:7,11; 11:25, etc.)? On the purely philological level, it could mean either. Relying on such Pauline interpretive passages as 1 Cor 11:26–29, early Christian tradition interpreted the verb in the former, realistic sense. It was only in the Middle Ages that this realistic sense began to be questioned. However, that sense, which is a distinct philological possibility, means that Jesus would have identified the bread and the wine with his own body and blood.

h. In some of the accounts Jesus' words include an interpretive element, which adds a soteriological dimension to the Eucharist. Whereas the Marcan and Matthean formulas simply identify the bread with Jesus' body, 1 Cor 11:24 adds, ". . . my body, *which is for you*" (a later [harmonizing?] correction is found in some Pauline manuscripts: "which is *broken* for you"); and Luke 22:19b has ". . . my body, which is *given for you*." Similarly, in the case of the cup of wine, the Pauline formula is the simplest (including a reference to the covenant in the identifying words). But the Synoptic formulas all agree at least in adding the interpretive words about the blood being "poured out for" (you/many). In both instances (of the words over the bread and over the cup of wine) one would be inclined to regard the leaner (Pauline) form as the more primitive (and possibly original), whereas the expanded forms would find a plausible matrix in the early Church's reflection on the significance of the eucharistic elements as related to the death of Jesus (i.e., added by hindsight from the vantage of post-resurrection faith in him). The soteriological aspect of Jesus' whole life and ministry was already part of the pre-Pauline kerygma (1 Cor 15:3 ["Christ died for our sins" (note the same preposition "for," *hyper*]; Rom 4:25 ["he was put to death for our trespasses and raised for our justification"]; 1 Thess 1:10). Whether or not we can answer the historical question about what formula Jesus actually used at the "Last Supper," the New Testament references to the institution of the Eucharist by him on that occasion have, in one form or another, associated such a soteriological connotation with it.

i. The perennial question emerges about the extent to which these words of Jesus reflect an awareness of his own destiny and of the giving of his life vicariously as a sacrifice for others. The discussion in the preceding section reveals an answer to that question in the sense that in the early Christian community his words were already so *understood.* Against the background of Exod 24:3–8 (the sacrificial ratification of the covenant of Sinai with the use of blood), the reference to the "blood of the covenant," present in some way in each formula used over the cup of wine, enhances the identification of the wine with Jesus' blood with the added sacrificial connotation. This much of an interpretive meaning may be traced back to Jesus himself—in some form. But these words reveal how difficult it is to separate the intention of his "very words" (*ipsissima verba*) from the interpreted intention of the subsequent tradition or of the evangelist's redaction. There is no solid reason to think that a soteriological, vicarious intention is not to be traced to what Jesus said over the bread and the wine at the "Last Supper." But there is simply no way of being certain about what went on in the mind of the historical Jesus on that occasion as he faced the prospect of death. We should all love to be able to answer such a question definitively; but who can—apart from a definitive intervention of the magisterium? (However, this is precisely the type of question in which the magisterium has not yet intervened and is unlikely to.)

Here once again it is important to realize that the twentieth-century Christian's faith in the Eucharist does not depend on what he/she can reconstruct of the words of the historical Jesus, but rather on the words as reflected to us through the early Christian community which recorded its diverse, varied recollections of him and of his impact on them in this matter. See §12 below.

j. In some of the New Testament accounts the early Church has passed on to us a tradition about Jesus' expectation that his followers were to re-enact the "Last Supper" as a rite among themselves—in memory of him (recall the memento-directive of 1 Cor 11:24–25; Luke 22:19c). Nothing is said, however, of this expectation in the Marcan or Matthean passages. The Church's eventual understanding of that rite as "sacramental" is rooted in what Jesus did and said at the "Last Supper." But none of the New Testament texts depict him associating this specific sacramental understanding with his words or actions. Rather, it took time for the Christian community to come to an awareness of this aspect of what he had done.

Similarly, the Pauline passage, being restricted to a brief recital of the essentials (in view of the argument which Paul was making), says nothing about who was at table with Jesus "on the night he was betrayed." The Synoptic narratives, however, provide some details about the occasion. The Marcan account portrays Jesus eating the "Last Supper" with the Twelve (14:17); the Matthean account is similar ("with the twelve disciples," 26:20). Luke also tells us of his sitting at table with "the apostles" (22:14), the name given to the Twelve in Luke 6:13. The memento-directive, recorded in the Pauline and Lucan accounts, would have been directed, then, to these select disciples. But in what sense? To them only? Or to them as representatives of all Jesus' followers? Was the supper to be re-enacted only during the lifetime of the Twelve, or even after them? We can answer the last question by arguing from what Paul says when he speaks of the eucharistic rite as a way of proclaiming the Lord's death "until he comes" (1 Cor 11:26). Those Pauline words, which scarcely envisage an imminent parousia, see the eucharistic rite as a way of proclaiming the soteriological death of Jesus the risen Lord. Those words imply that the re-enactment of the "Last Supper" was not to be limited to the first generation of Christian disciples. Their successsors were to continue it too. But who among them was to re-enact it? There is no way of telling from what we have inherited from the early Church's retelling of the "Last Supper" what might have been Jesus' intention in this regard. See further R. E. Brown, *Priest and Bishop: Biblical Reflections* (Paramus/New York: Paulist, 1970) 40–45. Thus the New Testament data regarding the "Last Supper" leave far more things open than most twentieth-century Christians would suspect.

11. Who Was Responsible for the Death of Jesus?

Literary evidence and new archaeological discoveries have often been invoked in recent times to serve as a background for the interpretation of the Gospel accounts about the interrogation and trial of Jesus of Nazareth. Passages in the writings of Josephus, of the Qumran sect, of rabbinical literature, and even of the apocryphal gospels have been used along with inscriptions and older material from Roman historians to shed some light on the Gospel accounts themselves. But no combination of this material has yet yielded a satisfying answer to the question about the responsibility for the death of Jesus.

a. The New Testament itself, which is the primary source of information about his interrogation, trial, and death, points an accusing finger at both Roman authority and Jewish leadership in Palestine of the time. It makes this accusation, however, with varying degrees of emphasis, depending on the individual New Testament writers. Modern Christians tend not to notice this variance of emphasis, but it has to be stressed.

b. The most extreme accusation is found in the earliest writing of the New Testament, in Paul's First Letter to the Thessalonians. There he speaks of "the Jews" (without any distinction) "who killed the Lord Jesus" (2:14–15); no mention is made of the Romans. This passage has often been regarded as the most anti-Semitic (in the modern sense of the adjective) in the Christian Bible.

c. In the passion narratives of the Gospels one can detect a tendency to inculpate the Jewish leaders and to exculpate the Roman prefect, Pontius Pilate. This tendency becomes evident, not in any one Gospel itself, but as the Gospel tradition grows and as one compares the treatment of the two parties in the four Gospels. Thus, in the earliest passion narrative, the responsibility is shared by chief priests, elders, and scribes of the Jewish people (Mark 14:1,43,53,55; 15:1,11) and by Pilate (15:15, "wishing to satisfy the crowd").

d. In the Matthean passion narrative the presentation differs little from the Marcan details (see 26:3,47,57,59; 27:1,62). This is because the Matthean passion narrative follows the Marcan so closely. But there are peculiarly Matthean additions which clearly modify the picture of Pilate's role: (i) His wife warns him to have nothing to do "with that innocent man" (27:19); (ii) Pilate washes his hands and declares openly his non-involvement: "I am innocent of the blood of this man; see to it yourselves. And all the people answered, 'His blood be upon us and upon our children'" (27:24–25).

e. In the Lucan passion narrative, which depends on the Marcan but is independent of the Matthean, the tendency is continued, but in a different way. Luke takes pains to distinguish "the people" or "the crowd" (22:2; 23:27,35a,48) from "the leaders" or the "elders, chief priests, and scribes" (22:2,52,54; 23:1,4,13,35b,51). Moreover, he omits all reference to false-witnesses or to accusations about the destruction of the temple, presenting Jesus rather as accused by the leaders solely of political agitation (23:2,5,18–19). Pilate is here depicted declaring Jesus innocent three times over (23:4,14–15,22). When he finally gives in, Luke makes it clear that "their voices prevailed; so Pilate gave sentence that their demand (for Barabbas) be granted . . . but Jesus he delivered to *their will*" (23:23–25). Verse 26 continues, "And as they led him away (to crucifixion). . . ." Here the "they" can refer only to the immediately preceding "their" (v. 25) or to the remote "chief priests and rulers of the people" (v. 13). It is only at v. 36 that (Roman) soldiers appear! And they mock Jesus as "the king of the Jews."

f. Finally, in the Johannine Gospel what was emerging in the Lucan passion narrative comes to even clearer expression. The council of chief priests and Pharisees gather against Jesus and discuss his effect on the people and the likely reaction of the Romans (11:47–53); Caiaphas is made to say, "It is expedient that one man should die for the people and that the whole nation should not perish" (v. 50). Then soldiers and officers from the chief priests and Pharisees deal with Judas (18:3,12–14 [here, however, some commentators try to see a reference to Romans in vv. 3,12; see R. E. Brown, *Gospel according to John XIII–XXI* (AB 29A; Garden City, N.Y.: Doubleday, 1970) 807–13]; the Johannine tradition is here at least ambiguous). When Jesus is finally brought before Pilate, he is again declared to be innocent three times over by the prefect (18:38; 19:4,6), who seeks to free him (18:31; 19:12). But when Pilate finally yields, the evangelist records, "Then he handed him over to them to be crucified" (19:16), where "them" in the context can refer only to "the chief priests" of v. 15. Verse 17 continues, "So they took Jesus; and he went out, bearing his own cross."

g. This comparison of details about the involvement of Pilate and Jewish leaders in the canonical passion narratives reveals a tendency at work in these writings which gradually makes the Jewish leaders more and more responsible for the death of Jesus. This tendency is carried forward in apocryphal writings such as the *Gospel of Peter*, where Pilate, seeing that none of the Jews, "neither Herod nor any of his judges would agree to wash their hands," as he had symbolically done, walks out on them. "Then Herod the king commanded that the Lord should be marched off" (§1–2; see E. Hennecke—W. Schneemelcher, *New Testament Apocrypha* [ed. R. M. Wilson; London: Lutterworth, 1959], 1. 183). And when Joseph of Arimathea later asks Pilate for Jesus' body, Pilate has to beg for it from Herod (§3–5). Thus Pilate gradually becomes "the good guy."

h. It is generally recognized that the tendency thus detected in the canonical passion narratives and the apocryphal *Gospel of Peter* undoubtedly reflects an attitude of early Christians who lived in various parts of the Roman empire and had to achieve recognition in it and seek for a *modus vivendi* within it. Christianity sought to be acknowledged in the empire as a *religio licita* (to borrow a term of later vintage), and this meant defining its relationship at once toward both Judaism (already so recognized) and the empire. No one can document this attitude or even the effort to play down Pilate's own involvement in the death of Jesus more precisely from other evidence than what we have presented here. Yet the tendency mentioned led in time to the notorious patristic and medieval charges of deicide leveled against the Jewish people. To cite but two examples: "Therefore the blood of Jesus came not only upon those who then lived, but upon all generations of Jews who followed thereafter even to the end (of the world)" (Origen, *Comm. in Matt. ser.* 124; PG 13. 1775); "And therefore the Jews sinned, not only as crucifiers of the man Christ, but also of God" (Thomas Aquinas, *S.T.* 3.47,5). This tendency, of course, complicates the attempt to answer the question originally posed.

i. In modern times attempts have been made to compare the details in the passion narratives with regulations in the *Mishnah,* the nucleus and earliest part of the rabbinical writings. Its sixty-three tractates, quoting the sayings of the Fathers, i.e., the rabbis of various generations, were compiled under R. Judah the Prince at the beginning of the third century A.D. and reduced to writing. The tractate *Sanhedrin* contains various regulations about capital punishment and lawsuits dealing with it (e.g., 4:1; see H. Danby, *The Mishnah* [Oxford: Oxford University, 1933] 386–87). Attempts have been made to show that the interrogation of Jesus by Jewish leaders as portrayed in the Gospels could never have taken place as recorded, or that the interrogation violates the regulations for due juridical process in Jewish *Mishnah.* Such comparison, however, leads nowhere, since neither set of writings, neither the Christian Gospels nor the Jewish traditions compiled in the *Mishnah* in post-New-Testament times, can be taken as historical documents of the sort that would permit a competent judgment or a valid answer to be given to the question posed. The discrepancies between the Synoptic accounts of the interrogation (one or two? at night or in the morning?) cannot be minimized. But it is equally impossible to establish that the idyllic regulations for judicial procedure recorded in the tractate *Sanhedrin* were actually in vogue in pre-70 Palestine. Both the *Mishnah* and the

Gospels are religious writings, composed for purposes other than answering historical questions such as the one posed.

j. Finally, the *Acts of Pilate,* which purports to be an account of Jesus' trial sent by the prefect to the emperor Tiberius in Rome, are manifestly a Christian composition of later date; they are devoid of any reliability as an independent historical testimony.

k. In recent times the thesis has often been proposed that only the Romans were responsible for the death of Jesus. It has been claimed that Palestinian Jewish authorities did not crucify or were incompetent to execute criminals, given the Roman occupation of the country at that time and the reservation of capital punishment to the occupiers (see John 18:31). There is, indeed, reason to acknowledge that the power of execution under the Romans was restricted. But it is far from clear that crucifixion was never employed by Jews in Palestine. The Hasmonean king Alexander Janneus (103–76 B.C.) crucified eight hundred of his enemy Jews (Josephus, *Ant.* 13.14,2 §380; *J.W.* 1.4,5–6 §93–98), and the recently published Temple Scroll from Qumran Cave 11 speaks clearly of crimes that call for such punishment (see 11QTemple 64:6–13; cf. my article, "Crucifixion in Ancient Palestine, Qumran Literature, and the New Testament," *CBQ* 40 [1978] 493–513, esp. pp. 503–04).

As a result, we cannot prove that some Jewish leaders of occupied Palestine or that Pilate and the Romans were *solely* responsible for the death of Jesus. Yet there is no real evidence to show that the general picture of the passion narratives, which implicates both parties, is wholly untrustworthy.

12.   Are There Different Interpretations of Jesus as the Christ (or Different Christologies) in the New Testament?

There are, indeed, and the sooner that readers of the New Testament learn to respect them, the better their comprehension of the New Testament will become. The tendency in the past to harmonize the data has been the cause of much misunderstanding about Jesus and his status as the God-man.

As already intimated (see §4d above), the "christology" of Jesus' earthly ministry can only be considered implicit or indirect. He sowed seeds during his ministry for what came to be recognized about him. What we call a "christology" today—the abstract term goes beyond the New Testament—is the product of a reflex mode of thought which makes explicit what New Testament writers had only partly formulated. Indeed, the affirmations about Jesus may have already made more explicit what was only implicit in his words, conduct, and teaching. But the christology of Paul, Luke, or John is a modern synthesis of what these New Testament writers have often left only concretely stated. To put it another way, one has to learn to respect the differences among the Pauline Christ Jesus, the Lucan Lord and Savior, and the Johannine Word-made-flesh.

It is impossible to spell out here all the details of the different New Testament christologies, but a few broad strokes may highlight some of the nuances that are to be respected.

a. Some New Testament books have relatively little christology. For example, the Epistle of James mentions Christ only twice (1:1; 2:1), "the Lord Jesus Christ," once in the opening address of the letter to identify the supposed author, and once to mention him in whom one is to put one's faith. Apart from the title "Lord," there is scarcely an affirmation about who he really is for the author.

b. In Paul's letters, the earliest New Testament writings, we find little that could be considered constitutive or ontological christology, because Paul is more interested in interpreting the significance of Christ Jesus for human beings than in telling us what Jesus was, what he did, or what he said.

Paul hints at the pre-existence of Christ by adopting a primitive Christian hymn and making it part of an exhortation in Phil 2:6–11. He speaks, moreover, of Christ as God's "Son" (Rom 1:3; 8:32) and even suggests something about his ontological relationship to "God the Father," precisely as "the Son himself" in 1 Cor 15:24–28. This

Questions

passage cannot be understood solely in a functional way, because in it the Son's role and relation to humanity and all creation is presumed to have come to an end: "Then comes the end, when he delivers the kingdom to God the Father after destroying every rule and every authority and power. . . . When all things are subjected to him, then *the Son himself* will also be subjected to him who put all things under him, that God may be everything to everyone" (vv. 24, 28). Christ's salvific role will have been terminated, and in its termination he will still be recognized in his essential relation as Son of the Father.

Paul uses, indeed, explicit christological titles (e.g., Lord, Son of God, Messiah), but he is really far more interested in soteriology than in christology as such. His letters are replete with modes of describing the effects of the Christ-event, what Christ Jesus has done for mankind in his ministry, passion, death, burial, resurrection, exaltation, and heavenly intercession. When Paul looks back at that complex, he attributes to it a "once-for-all" character (*ephapax,* Rom 6:10); he sees it under various images reflecting not only his own Jewish and Hellenistic backgrounds, but also the controversies and debates of his missionary experience.

He sees the effect of that complex at times as "salvation" (Rom 1:16; 5:9; 10:10), "justification" (Gal 2:16–21; Rom 3:21–26; 4:25), "reconciliation" (2 Cor 5:18–20; Rom 5:10–11; 11:15), "redemption/ ransom" (Rom 3:24; 8:23), "freedom" (Gal 5:1,13; 2 Cor 3:17; Rom 8:2), "transformation/metamorphosis" (2 Cor 3:16–18; Rom 12:2), "new creation" (Gal 6:15; 2 Cor 5:17), "expiation" (Rom 3:25), "new life" (1 Cor 15:45; Rom 6:4), "adoptive sonship" (Gal 4:4–6; Rom 8:14–16), "sanctification" (1 Cor 1:30; 6:11), and possibly "forgiveness/pardon" of sins (Rom 3:25 [*paresis,* of disputed meaning]; Col 1:14 and Eph 1:7 [of disputed Pauline authorship]). Only Johannine soteriology and christology, distinctive with its own emphases, can come near to the richness of the Pauline view of Christ Jesus.

c. Lucan christology seems to include neither incarnation nor pre-existence; these notions are not found in either the Third Gospel or Acts. It knows of Jesus' exaltation/ascension, but is silent about his heavenly intercession. It makes abundant use of early explicit titles (Messiah, Lord, Savior, Son, Prophet, Servant, Son of Man, Teacher), but also has some which are exclusively Lucan: suffering Messiah (Luke 24:26,46; Acts 3:18; 17:3; 26:23), author of life (Acts 3:15; 5:31), Messiah designate (Acts 3:20), and holy and righteous one (Acts 3:14). Luke too has a way of looking back at the effects of the Christ-event, but in contrast to the multiple images employed by Paul, he sums up his soteriology only under a few figures: "salvation" (Luke 2:30; Acts 13:26; alone among the Synoptic evangelists, Luke calls Jesus "Savior," 2:11; cf. Acts 5:31; 13:23); "forgiveness of sins" (*aphesis,* Luke 24:47; Acts 13:38), "Peace" (Luke 2:14; 19:42; Acts 10:36), and "justification" (Acts 13:39 [but with a nuance different from the Pauline understanding of it]).

d. Johannine christology, however, moves with a much deeper understanding of explicit christology. It insists on understanding Jesus as one in whom God is seen among human beings and in whom God's salvation is now concretized in a totally new way. Jesus in his person replaces the presence of God-among-men of old (the *shĕ kînāh*-idea) and the institutions of Judaism (the temple, the ritual washings, the manna as the bread of life). Johannine christology is "high," including the incarnation of the Word, the identification of the Son with the Father in their concern for the world, and even elements of a relational, ontological christology (the Word was not only with God, but was God, 1:1). It is to be noted that the Jesus of the Johannine Gospel, all during his earthly ministry, speaks as if he were already in glory; because of this, the Johannine Jesus makes such statements as "Before Abraham was, I am" (8:58); "I and the Father are one" (10:30). Such statements as these, put on Jesus' lips by the Fourth Evangelist, are precisely the building-blocks of the "high" christology that one meets in the Johannine writings and that make it so different from that of other New Testament writings.

This christology, however, co-exists along with a number of explicit titles derived from the earlier tradition: Messiah (even explained as "Christ," 1:41), Son of God (1:34), Teacher (1:38, as a translation of rabbi), King of Israel (12:13), Son of Man (1:51; 3:13, etc.), Prophet (4:19), Savior (4:42 [shared with Luke]). But it also has a number of its own titles: "Lamb of God" (1:29,36); "good Shepherd" (10:11); "Bread of life" (6:35,51). These exclusively Johannine titles are more expressive of soteriology than of christology. The effects of the Christ-event in the Johannine view are set forth under the following figures: "salvation" (3:17; 12:47), "taking away of sin" (1:29), "enlightenment" (1:9), "empowering" human beings "to become children of God" (1:12: 3:5–7), giving a "share in eternal life" (3:36; 4:14; 5:24), precisely through the "resurrection" (11:25–26).

e. Another whole area in which one would have to distinguish New Testament christologies is that of the relation of Jesus to the Spirit. Whereas Paul does not always clearly distinguish the risen Christ from the Spirit (e.g., 2 Cor 3:17: "The Lord is the Spirit"; cf. 1 Cor 15:45; Rom 1:4), there are triadic passages in his letters where the parallelism implies a distinction (such as 1 Cor 12:4–6; 2 Cor 13:14). The distinction, however, is made clear in both Lucan and Johannine christology (Luke 24:49; Acts 1:4; 2:4–21,33; John 7:39; 14:26; 15:26; 16:7–11).

f. As we have sketched here briefly the Pauline, Lucan, and Johannine christologies, we could also do the same for the Gospel according to Matthew, the Epistle to the Hebrews, and the Book of Revelation, three important New Testament writings, which have christologies of their own.

g. These differing christologies also reveal why it is difficult today to write a theology of the New Testament in the way that one used to attempt it. For if there are differing christologies, there are also differing theologies in the New Testament. They cannot be simply harmonized, and that is why it is wrong to interpret passages in the Gospels by Pauline ideas or sayings of Jesus in the Synoptics by nuances from the Johannine tradition. The different christologies in the New Testament amount to different portraits of Jesus that the early Christian community has sketched of him and left behind as its heritage to feed the faith of subsequent generations and centuries of Christian believers.

h. If our answers to questions 1 and 2 above were somewhat negative and minimal, it is good to remember that the faith of modern Christians is not measured by what they can establish about the historical Jesus of Nazareth. Faith in the twentieth century means an allegiance to him who entered human history as God's agent and Son, but also to him as reflected and refracted in the experience and tradition of the early Christian community. This is not to put a book (the New Testament) between Jesus and the modern believer, or even the christologies of the early Christians between them. However, the *inspired christologies* are normative of Christian faith, in a sense, in a way in which none of the later tradition is. The twentieth-century Christian has no pipeline to him apart from or independent of these writings and these christologies, different as they are. Two things have to be kept in tandem, Jesus of Nazareth and the early Christian portraits of him. These are the *norma normans* of all later christological and soteriological teaching. This will be further developed as we proceed.

13. Does the Story of the Virgin Birth Record Simple Historical Fact or Are There Other Possible Ways of Understanding It?

First of all, for the sake of clarity in a discussion of New Testament data, it would be better to speak of the virginal *conception* of Jesus, because that is the only question at issue in the infancy narratives. We are concerned with what has been called Mary's *virginitas ante partum*, "virginity before the birth (of Jesus)." Nothing is said in the New Testament about the mode of Mary's *giving birth* to Jesus, i.e., about what came to be called later *virginitas in partu*, "virginity in the (actual) birth." The expression "virgin birth" has come into modern parlance because of the simple way in which the creeds of the early Church formulated their affirmation ("natus est de Spiritu Sancto ex Maria virgine"; *ton gennēthenta ek pneumatos hagiou kai Marias tēs parthenou*).

a. The virginal conception of Jesus is never referred to by Paul, Mark, or the Johannine tradition; among New Testament writers the only ones who touch upon it are Matthew and Luke. Paul knows of Jesus' Davidic descent (Rom 1:3) and stresses Jesus' birth "from a woman" (Gal 4:4) in a fundamentally soteriological statement. He knows of Jesus' divine sonship and implies his pre-existence (see §12b above); neither of these details is considered by him to be in conflict with the two preceding facts.

Mark has no infancy narrative, and there is not the slightest trace of a belief in the virginal conception in his Gospel. Because it is usually thought that the infancy narratives were the last part of the Gospel tradition to take shape, the narrative about the virginal conception in the Matthean and Lucan Gospels represents almost certainly a post-Marcan development.

Even though the Johannine Gospel is the latest in its final redaction among the canonical Gospels, its tradition in part may go back to a period as early as that of the earliest Synoptic (Mark). But, significantly, it shows no knowledge of the developed conception-christology which manifests itself in the infancy narratives of Matthew and Luke. (The reader should not be misled by the reading of John 1:13 in *The Jerusalem Bible,* which follows a patristic tradition: "who was born not out of human stock or urge of the flesh or will of man, but of God himself." This reading suggests the virginal conception, but it is not supported by any Greek manuscript of the Fourth Gospel or found in any modern critical text of the Greek New Testament!)

b. The virginal conception of Jesus is recounted in the Matthean and Lucan infancy narratives. It is clearly asserted in Matt 1:18–25 and, perhaps less clearly, in Luke 1:31–35. In both the Matthean and Lucan infancy narratives the evangelist intends to tell us who Jesus is and whence he comes. Through the genealogy and the angel's message to Joseph, Matthew gets across Jesus' Davidic descent and the Spirit's role in his conception; Luke presents the same two ideas, both of them in the message of Gabriel to Mary. In both of these episodes we may detect a dramatization and Christian development of a christological affirmation which was once stated merely in a parallelism in the kerygmatic fragment embedded in Rom 1:3–4: "descended from David according to the flesh and constituted Son of God in power according to a spirit of holiness as of (his) resurrection from the dead." What was kerygmatically proclaimed about Jesus' relation to David and to the Spirit (as of the resurrection) was in time pressed back to his very conception in the tradition which both Matthew and Luke inherited from the Christian community before them. The Marcan Gospel, which lacks an infancy narrative, used the baptism scene (1:10–11) to express a similar relationship of Jesus to God involving the Spirit. This relationship constitutes the major doctrinal affirmation of the Matthean and Lucan stories of the virginal conception of Jesus; their main thrust is an affirmation about Jesus, not about Mary.

c. Neither the Lucan nor the Matthean infancy narrative reckons with the pre-existence or incarnation of Christ. These elements of a "high" (or highly developed) christology may have been at home in an earlier stage of the New Testament tradition (e.g., see Phil 2:6–11 and the comments made above in §12b). But the christology of the infancy narratives is "higher" than the Marcan in presenting Jesus' relation to God through the Spirit as something now realized to be true of his very conception.

d. What we have said so far sums up the matter of Jesus' conception in terms of christological assertion—or, as some prefer to call it, as a theologoumenon, or possibly as a *Glaubensaussage,* "affirmation of faith." That it certainly is. It is possible to understand the virginal conception of Jesus, as described in the New Testament, solely in this way (recall the wording of the question). But is the account of the virginal conception also intended as an affirmation of "historical fact"? It has, indeed, been so understood by New Testament interpreters (e.g., H. Schürmann, who would trace it to an "intimate family tradition"); it has been understood as historical and based in part on a public knowledge of Mary's early pregnancy before she came to live with Joseph (see Matt 1:18c)—but how would that public have come to know of it "as of the Holy Spirit"? In this matter, which needs far more discussion than space permits here, one can only say, with R. E. Brown, that "the *scientifically controllable* biblical evidence leaves the question of the historicity of the virginal conception unresolved." But Brown also acknowledges that for Roman Catholics the long-standing Church tradition supplies an answer to that part of the question.

e. It is good to recall that even in the Gospels which have an infancy narrative and assert the virginal conception of Jesus there are elements of a tradition which either do not reckon with it or have not been integrated into such a belief. For instance, Luke 2:41 speaks of Mary and Joseph as "his parents" (cf. v. 43), and Mary says to the twelve-year-old Jesus, "Your father and I have been looking for you" (2:48). This is simply said, with no qualification such as "foster father" or "putative father." And Matt 13:55 records the query, "Is not this the carpenter's son?" Cf. John 6:42.

f. In sum, one has to recognize that the New Testament data for this question are not unambiguous; they do not necessarily support the claim that this belief was a matter of "the constant teaching of the Church from the beginning" (M. Schmaus, "Mariology," *Sacramentum mundi* [New York: Herder and Herder, 1968–70), 3. 379. The data suggest rather that this belief became part of the developing christology of the early Church, within New Testament times.

In this matter one should consult R. E. Brown, *The Birth of the Messiah* (Garden City, N.Y.: Doubleday, 1977) 517–33; R. E. Brown et al. (eds.), *Mary in the New Testament: A Collaborative Assessment by Protestant and Roman Catholic Scholars* (New York: Paulist; Philadelphia: Fortress, 1978) 74–134; and my article, "The Virginal Conception of Jesus in the New Testament," *TS* 34 (1973) 541–75, now reprinted with a postscript in *To Advance the Gospel: New Testament Studies* (New York: Crossroad, 1981) 41–78.

14. How Are We To Understand the Reference to the Brothers and Sisters of Jesus in the New Testament?

The main references to Jesus' brothers and sisters in the New Testament are found in the episode of Jesus' visit to "his own country" (Mark 6:1–3): "Is not this the carpenter, the son of Mary and brother of James and Joses and Judas and Simon, and are not his sisters here with us?" Cf. Matt 13:55–56, which has a slightly different formulation. See also Mark 3:32; Matt 12:46. The Johannine tradition mentions "his mother and brothers" (2:12), but also records that "his brothers" did not believe in him (7:5). Likewise, Paul knows of James of Jerusalem as "a brother of the Lord" (Gal 1:19; recall Josephus' echo of this tradition, quoted in §2 above). Do these references mean "blood brothers and sisters, siblings" or are they to be understood otherwise?

a. Some interpreters, recalling the long tradition about Mary as *aeiparthenos* or "semper virgo" (DS 44, 46), prefer to understand the phrases in a broader sense; on the other hand, many Protestant interpreters understand them to mean blood brothers or sisters. The perpetual virginity of Mary is well attested in the third century, and by implication is already found in the second-century writing, *Protevangelium Jacobi* (Hennecke-Schneemelcher, *New Testament Apocrypha,* 1. 374–88 esp. 9:2; 17:1; 18:1 [children of Joseph from a former marriage]; see *Mary in the New Testament,* 273–75). But the question is complicated by the New Testament evidence itself; the answer rests not on the later ecclesiastical tradition alone.

b. Matt 1:25 has to be interpreted carefully: "He [Joseph] knew her not until (*heōs* [*hou*]) she had borne a son." This has often been thought to mean that Mary's virginity was preserved until the birth of Jesus (*virginitas ante partum*), but that after it Joseph had intercourse with her. A careful analysis of the passage (vv. 18–25) reveals that Matthew's primary interest was in what preceded the birth of Jesus and in its relation to Isa 7:14 (LXX: a virgin who conceives and bears a son). Verse 25, then, asserts that Mary remained a virgin even until Jesus was born. It says nothing about any marital relations after the birth of Jesus. It is only when Matt 1:25 is read in conjunction with Mark 6:1–3 or Matt 13:55–56 that one begins to ask whether something more may be implied there. *Per se,* however, Matt 1:25 does not imply *virignitas post partum* (virginity after the birth [of Jesus]), nor does it deny it. The whole issue raises a further question about how dependent the traditions in the infancy narrative were on the rest of the traditions of that Gospel.

c. It is well known that Greek *adelphos* may mean something more than merely "blood brother" (e.g., "co-religionist" [Rom 9:3], "neighbor" [Matt 5:22–24], "step-brother" [Mark 6:17–18], "kinsman, relative" [Gen 29:12; 24:48]—in the last sense it merely reflects the broad sense of Hebrew *'āh* or Aramaic *'ăha'*). The question is whether this sense of "relative, kinsman" could possibly have been meant in the phrases of Mark 6:1–3. Is there any basis in the New Testament for so understanding it? (N.B. The New Testament has a word for "cousin" [Col 4:10, *anepsios*]; so this meaning should not be foisted on *adelphos.*)

d. Mark 15:40 supplies a reason for raising the question about the meaning of *adelphos.* It lists the three women standing at a distance from the cross and looking at the crucified Jesus: Mary Magdalene, Mary the mother of James the younger and of Joses, and Salome. It is hardly likely that the evangelist would be using such a circumlocution as "Mary the mother of James and Joses" to designate the mother of the person hanging on the cross. He would have almost certainly said "his mother" or "the mother of Jesus." Moreover, it is only in the Johannine tradition that it is said that "his mother" was standing by the cross (19:25). The Synoptic tradition knows nothing of this. But since the sons James and Joses are two of the *adelphoi* mentioned in Mark 6:3, the question is then raised: In what sense is *adelphos* used there? If it means "blood brother," then it would imply that Mark was using a strange circumlocution to say that Mary, the mother of Jesus, was standing at a distance from the cross. But if the phrase in 15:40 does not refer to the mother of the crucified Jesus, then Mark 15:40 would seem to suggest that *adelphos* in 6:3 is to be understood in a sense other than "blood brother," e.g., "relative, kinsman." See also Mark 15:47; 16:1; cf. Matt 27:56,61; 28:1.

In other words the New Testament itself is ambiguous about the meaning of *adelphos* in Mark 6:3, when that verse is compared with Mark 15:40,47; 16:1. This ambiguity bears then on the question of Mary's perpetual virginity. It means that one cannot solve easily, on the basis of the New Testament evidence alone, the question whether Jesus' "brothers and sisters" have to be understood in the strict sense of siblings or in the broad sense of kinsmen, relatives. The latter possibility is certainly not ruled out.

15. How Do Contemporary New Testament Interpreters Deal with the Resurrection of Jesus?

The resurrection of Jesus is the cardinal affirmation of Christian faith found in the New Testament and passed on to us by early Christians. To confess that "Jesus is Lord," one has to admit that "God raised him from the dead" (Rom 10:9) and that "if Christ has not been raised, then is our preaching in vain and your faith in vain too" (1 Cor 15:14). Not to admit the resurrection of Jesus means that one is not a Christian.

a. The problem which modern readers of the New Testament have with the resurrection of Jesus is not so much the basic Christian kerygma (enshrined in such passages as 1 Cor 15:3–7; 1 Thess 1:9–10; Rom 4:25) as with either the resurrection narratives of the Gospel tradition or the way in which they tend to imagine to themselves what the New Testament has to say about the risen Jesus.

b. First of all, one has to reckon with six different resurrection narratives in the New Testament:

(i) Mark 16:1–8, which is the conclusion of the Marcan Gospel in the best Greek manuscripts of that Gospel (Vaticanus, Sinaiticus). (Three other endings are found in some manuscripts: (1) the canonical Marcan appendix, vv. 9–20, found in the Koine text-tradition and codices A, C, D, W, L, etc. [see vi below]; (2) an expanded v. 8 in codices L, 099, 0112, etc.; and (3) the so-called Freer Logion, added to v. 14 in codex Washingtonianus.) Verses 1–8 report the discovery of the empty tomb by the women, Mary Magdalene, Mary the mother of James, and Salome, and the *praeconium paschale,* "the Easter proclamation," that "he has been raised; he is not here" (v. 6c), as well as the silence and withdrawal of the women, "for they were afraid" (*ephobounto gar*—with a conjunction forming the strange ending of a biblical book!). These Marcan verses have no description of the resurrection itself nor any appearances of the risen Jesus, but they do promise that Peter and others will see him in Galilee.

(ii) Matt 28:1–20, which likewise reports the discovery of the empty tomb and the Easter message, "He is not here, for he has been raised, as he said" (vv. 1–8). But this narrative includes an appearance of the risen Christ in Jerusalem to the women, to Mary Magdalene and the other Mary (vv. 9–10), the report and bribery of the guard by the chief priests and elders (vv. 11–15), another appearance of Christ to the Eleven in Galilee (vv. 16–17), and his commission to them to make other disciples by teaching and baptism (vv. 18–20).

(iii) Luke 24:1–53, which also tells of the finding of the empty tomb and of the Easter message, "He is not here, but has been raised" (vv. 1–12), but also of appearances of the risen Christ at Emmaus (vv. 13–35) and in Jerusalem (vv. 36–43), of his commission to his disciples to be "witnesses of these things" (vv. 44–49), and of his ascension (vv. 50–53).

(iv) John 20:1–29, which records the finding of the empty tomb (vv. 1–10) and recounts the appearance of the risen Christ to Mary Magdalene (vv. 11–18), to disciples in Jerusalem (with Thomas, one of the Twelve, absent, vv. 19–23), and again to disciples (with Thomas present, vv. 24–29).

(v) The Johannine appendix (21:1–23), which resumes the narrative after the concluding verses of 20:30–31 and tells only of Jesus' appearance to seven disciples in Galilee (with the contrasting roles of Peter and the beloved disciple set forth).

(vi) The Marcan appendix (16:9–20), which is found only in some Greek manuscripts [see above] and reports three appearances of Jesus in Jerusalem or its environs on Easter Sunday (vv. 9–11,12–13,14–18) and his "being taken up" on that same day.

c. In contrast to the notable parallelism among the four passion narratives, the resurrection narratives go their own ways, save for the four accounts of the discovery of the empty tomb and two verses in the Marcan appendix (16:12–13), which may refer to the Emmaus incident (Luke 24:13–35). This diversity of appearance-stories is puzzling: Why should there not have been more agreement among them, or at least of them with the list of witnesses recorded in 1 Cor 15:5–7? Even the "great commission," present in Matt 28:18–20; Luke 24:47–49; Mark 16:15–16, is in each Gospel actually suited to the theological thrust of that writing (even in the Marcan appendix!).

Moreover, the stories of Jesus' appearances are sometimes "concise" (to use C. H. Dodd's form-critical terminology), i.e., well-rounded and shaped by frequent repetition (e.g., Matt 28:8–10,16–20, John 20:19–23); sometimes they are dramatic or "circumstantial" tales (e.g., Luke 24:13–35; John 21:1–14), where the creative hand of the evangelist has been at work fashioning details and conversations and observing the unities of time and space; and sometimes they are "mixed," i.e., "concise" stories on their way to becoming "circumstantial" tales (e.g., Mark 16:14–15; Luke 24:36–43; John 20:11–18,24–29). In other words, the accounts of Jesus' appearances are the products of varying tradition and composition and are scarcely reflections of the earliest level of preaching about the risen Christ. By contrast, the earliest levels of the tradition speak at times of his "exaltation" to glory from his death on the cross, omitting all reference to the resurrection (see the pre-Pauline Christian hymn used in Phil 2:8–11; cf. 1 Tim 3:16, also a primitive piece used in a later writing). The resurrection narratives, with all their diversity, have to be seen as attempts to fill out the details of the reports of appearances of the risen Christ preserved in such fundamental proclamations as 1 Cor 15:3–7.

d. Was the tomb really found empty? This is not merely a modern question, since the Matthean Gospel reflects a Christian reaction to objections about it or to a question of this sort: 27:62–66 (the sealing of the tomb and the posting of the guard); 28:11–15 (the report of the guard and the bribing of them). These passages are peculiar to Matthew and bear the obvious marks of apologetics against "the Jews." But they are confined to one Gospel and scarcely account for every form of the story of the empty tomb (e.g., in the earlier Marcan narrative, or in the almost certainly independent Johannine tradition).

In the 1930's a first-century ossuary turned up in Jerusalem bearing the name of the deceased, *Yēshûa' bar Yĕhôsēph,* "Jesus son of Joseph." (An ossuary is a stone-box used for the "second burial" of the collected bones of a dead person after the flesh has decomposed.) The Jewish scholar who discovered the ossuary and published the inscription, E. L. Sukenik (the father of Y. Yadin, the former deputy prime-minister of Israel), drew no conclusions from it about any New Testament personage, realizing that "Jesus" and "Joseph" were commonly used names for Palestinian Jews in the first century. Such a discovery scarcely invalidated the story of the empty tomb.

It is sometimes argued, however, that Paul in the kerygmatic fragment used in 1 Cor 15:3–5 makes no mention of an empty tomb: "that Christ died for our sins according to the Scriptures, that he was buried, that he was raised on the third day according to the Scriptures, and that he appeared to Cephas, then to the Twelve. . . ." Hence, the story of the empty tomb would seem to be of later (apologetic) origin. True, the empty tomb is not mentioned in this kerygmatic passage. But here one has to reckon with the parallel four-item formulation of the first part of this fragment (death, burial, resurrection, appearances), which can also be found reflected in Paul's speech in Acts 13:28–31. Its formulaic character was clearly of greater value than the inclusion of all details. It may be that *narrative accounts* of the discovery of the empty tomb only came to be formulated later than the kerygma itself, but this later emergence does not really exclude all factuality itself.

e. The other modern problem with the resurrection of Jesus is the way in which we tend to picture to ourselves what the New Testament has passed on about the risen Christ. Here several important points should be recalled:

(i) Despite Acts 1:22, in the episode about the election of Matthias, which lists as a criterion for membership in the Twelve one who had been "a witness to the resurrection," no one witnessed the resurrection of Jesus. It is never so put, not even in Matt 28:2b, which does mention the earthquake and the angel of the Lord who descended, rolled back the stone of the tomb, and sat upon it. In Acts 1:22 Luke has formulated abstractly what was really meant: "a witness to the risen Christ" was to be the replacement of Judas, i.e., one to whom he had appeared (similarly for Acts 4:33). For none of the canonical Gospels attempts to do what the later apocryphal *Gospel of Peter* does (§35–42), i.e., describe the coming forth of Jesus from the tomb—which represents an effort to answer *later* queries about how it happened—or describes the resurrection as Luke does the ascension in Acts 1:9–11.

(ii) The New Testament never presents the resurrection of Jesus as a resuscitation, i.e., a return to his former mode of terrestrial existence (like that, say, of Lazarus, John 11:43–44; 12:1–2). Jesus is never portrayed inhabiting the earth for forty days or appearing as someone who had been ensconced behind an arras. Indeed, Luke 24:37–39 strives explicitly to reject the idea that he was like a spook.

(iii) Though the New Testament does not say so explicitly, it implies time and again that when the risen Christ appeared, he appeared from glory, i.e., from the presence of the Father. Rom 6:4 says that "Christ was raised from the dead by the glory of the Father." And the risen Christ asks the disciples on the road to Emmaus, "Did not the Christ have to suffer these things and *enter into his glory*?" (Luke 24:26). Moreover, the only difference between the appearance of the risen Christ to Paul on the road to Damascus and that to the others earlier was, in reality, a temporal one, i.e., it happened to Paul after Pentecost. This has to be recognized despite the Lucan differences of descriptive details. The "spatial" *terminus a quo* of the appearances should not be understood as different in these cases.

(iv) Whereas the risen Christ who appears to his disciples insists on his identity, he is also said to have appeared "in another form" (Marcan appendix, 16:12). He was at first recognized by neither Cleopas and his companion (Luke 24:16) nor Mary Magdalene (John 20:14–16). However one wants to explains this, one must recall in this connection Paul's admission that there is a difference between a "physical body" sown in death and a "spiritual body" raised therefrom (1 Cor 15:42–44). Indeed, when Paul tries to describe the risen body, he identifies it expressly with what is not "body," viz., "spirit(ual)." Are we to write that off simply as a rhetorical oxymoron? Scarcely. But it says something about how we should envision the risen Christ and his "glorified" body.

f. The kerygma of early Christianity, which proclaimed the death, burial, raising, and appearances of Christ, originated in a Palestinian Jewish-Christian setting, wherein the notion of the afterlife was not that of the Greek philosophical dichotomy of body/soul or the immortality of the soul. It arose in a milieu in which "resurrection" (see Dan 12:2) would only have been understood as a *bodily* resurrection. Perhaps we cannot explain just what such a view of afterlife would entail. But the early kerygma did not content itself to affirm merely that Jesus was alive or that he was a living influence in the lives of his followers. It included an admission that Jesus had been "raised" to a state of glory in the presence of the Father—and that would have had to mean "bodily."

Even though some biblical interpreters would like to dismiss the idea of a bodily resurrection of Jesus and are skeptical about the empty-tomb tradition, we must emphasize that the bodily resurrection of Jesus to glory is a basic part of the New Testament kerygmatic proclamation and a fundamental affirmation of Christian faith.

16. What Do Contemporary New Testament Interpreters Say of the Ascension?

a. In analyzing the different references in the New Testament to Jesus' ascension, we must reckon with their varying nuances.

i. The earliest references speak of Jesus' transit to the Father or to glory as an "exaltation" and use this term in a way which makes it difficult to be sure whether the resurrection or the ascension (or possibly both) is meant. These references seem to describe a passage from death on the cross to a heavenly existence with the Father in glory without mention of the resurrection (see Phil 2:8–11, part of the pre-Pauline hymn used there; the primitive hymn embedded in 1 Tim 3:16; recall also the Johannine mode of speaking about Jesus being "lifted up," e.g., 12.32–34).

ii. Some New Testament passages refer to the ascension without describing it or fixing it in time or place (e.g., Rom 10:6 [by implication]; more explicitly, Eph 4:8–10). In such passages, Christ's ascension is taken for granted and is used to make some other theological affirmation, e.g., the ease of Christian faith (Romans 10) or the bounty of the glorified Christ to the Christian community (Ephesians 4).

iii. Some New Testament passages refer to Jesus' being "carried up to heaven," being "taken up to heaven," or "ascending" to the Father on the day of the resurrection itself (Luke 24:51; the Marcan appendix, 16:19; John 20:17). These passages fix a date (Easter Sunday) and a term (heaven, the Father) for this transit. They closely relate the ascension to the event of Easter and thus differ only slightly from the mode of exaltation mentioned above in the first instance.

iv. Acts 1:3,9,11 gives a brief description of the transit, fixes it in time (some forty days after the resurrection [1:3]—but cf. Acts 13:31, simply "many days" [*hēmeras pleious*]), in space (from the Mount of Olives [1:12]), in a specific mode ("lifted up, with a cloud taking him out of sight" [1:9]), and in its term (heaven [1:11]). From this Lucan scene in Acts 1 we have derived the traditional mode of representing to ourselves the "ascension." This scene is the only New Testament passage, however, which does this and does what the apocryphal *Gospel of Peter* sought to do for the resurrection (see §15e above), i.e., depict Christ's coming out of the tomb. But Luke 24 has dated the "ascension" of Christ to Easter Sunday itself, in contrast to the date given in Acts 1. Scribes who later copied the codices Sinaiticus and Bezae and translator(s) of the *Vetus Latina* sought to solve the discrepancy by omitting the crucial words of Luke 24:51, "and he was carried up to heaven." In their critical edition of 1881, Westcott and Hort omitted these words and started a fad among New Testament textual critics. Since the discovery of Papyrus Bodmer XIV, however, which is the oldest papyrus text of the Lucan Gospel (dated A.D. 200 $\pm$ 25 years), most textual critics no longer agree with their judgment. For those words are found not only in that oldest papyrus text, but also in the vast majority of the best Greek manuscripts. Moreover, they represent a reading which copyists would more logically have omitted (to solve the discrepancy) than added (to create one). Those words of v. 51 are the *lectio difficilior praeferenda* (the text-critical principle of preferring the more difficult reading). See P. Benoit, "The Ascension," *Jesus and the Gospel: Volume 1* (New York: Herder and Herder, 1973) 209–53.

b. "Ascent/ascension" means motion upward, and implied in the New Testament accounts of Jesus' ascension is a movement through the heavens or the celestial spheres (see Eph 4:10; cf. Aristotle, *Metaphys.* 12.8 1073a). The transit to "the Father" or "to God" (John 20:17) has at times employed in the New Testament not only apocalyptic stage-props ("being taken up to heaven," with "a cloud" as a vehicle) but also made use of a time-conditioned sense of "heaven(s)." There is, moreover, a fluctuation in the terminology, between a passive assumption ("he was taken/carried up" [by God/the Father]) and an active ascension ("I am ascending" [John 20:17], "one who ascended" [Eph 4:8]). These time-conditioned elements and fluctuations create part of the difficulty in trying to understand what is really meant.

c. The "ascension" affirms for the Christian readers of the New Testament that the risen, exalted Christ is with the Father in glory (recall Luke 24:26), whence he sends the Spirit to his followers as a dynamic and effective mode of his presence among them, when he is no longer visibly manifest to them.

What is really at issue in the New Testament passages dealing with the "ascension" of Jesus is an attempt to describe the complex phase of his existence which we variously refer to as his resurrection, exaltation, ascension, or transit to the Father, along with his continued presence to his followers/Church in his life-giving Spirit. This complex is, in the proper sense, the "paschal mystery" (a term often abused today).

Once we realize that Jesus' resurrection has not been presented in the New Testament as a resuscitation or a return to terrestrial life or existence, but as a bodily resurrection to the glorious presence of the Father and that his appearances to his disciples were made from that glory, then his "ascension" is readily understood as his final appearance, as his visible leave-taking from his assembled followers. He would no longer so present himself to them in their corporate unity (not yet called "Church" in Acts). Henceforth, his "presence" among them would be through the Spirit, the "promise of my Father" (Luke 24:49; Acts 1:4), which he as one exalted to the right hand of God pours out (Acts 2:33). (He would also be present to them "in the breaking of the bread," as the Emmaus incident implies

[Luke 24:35].) True, the risen Christ does present himself later to
Saul of Tarsus on the road to Damascus, in a post-pentecostal appearance (Acts 9:5; 22:8, 26:15), where Luke recounts once in dramatic form and twice in speeches what Paul himself refers to in 1
Cor 9:1 and Gal 1:16 (without any reference to Pentecost). But that
was an appearance of the risen Christ to an individual "vessel of election" (Acts 9:15), especially chosen to become "the apostle of the
Gentiles" (Rom 11:13).

  d. Related to the "ascension" is the gift of the Spirit, as the last
paragraph implies. In Acts 2:4 the Spirit is "poured out" on Pentecost, fifty days after Passover (cf. 2:33). But in John 20:22 the Spirit
is given by the risen Christ to the assembled disciples on Sunday
night itself: "He breathed on them and said, 'Receive [the] Holy
Spirit.' " This discrepancy of date about the giving of the Spirit to
Christian disciples is similar to that of the "date" of the ascension,
although in this case it is not a discrepancy found within the writings
of the same New Testament author. We cannot resolve the question
about *when* the Spirit was first bestowed upon early Christians, any
more than we can date the "ascension." In either tradition (Lucan or
Johannine) the basic affirmation of the gift is common: a bestowal
which Paul, the earliest theologian of the New Testament, either affirms or takes for granted over and over again (Gal 3:2,5; 4:6; Rom
8:2–3,12–17; 1 Cor 12:3).

  It is Luke who, in his well-known concern to press home the *reality* of the risen Christ and of the Spirit in Christian life, has histori-
cized *phases* of the complex Christ-event and its effects. Facets of it
have been dramatized to stress the reality of the gift and the reality
of the presence and influence of the risen Christ.

17. Did Jesus Clearly Claim To Be God?

  This question could be asked with different nuances. If it is
meant as a query about the consciousness of the historical Jesus dur-

ing his earthly ministry, it faces the problems already mentioned in §2f above. We have no way of answering it in terms of what went on in his mind. The only documents that we have about what he did or said, which might reflect indirectly his awareness, were written at least a generation after his death. They scarcely reflect his direct or reflex consciousness in any explicit way. The Johannine Jesus says, "I and the Father are one" (10:30) or "The Father is in me and I am in the Father" (10:38). But the real question is whether one can appeal naively to such statements of the Johannine Jesus to answer the question posed in terms of his historical consciousness. One cannot ignore the Johannine context of such statements or the thrust of that Gospel as a whole. To give this sort of answer to the question would be to give misguided reassurance to the "fundamentalism of the fearful" (to use a recent phrase of Anglican Bishop John A. T. Robinson, *Can We Trust the New Testament?* [Grand Rapids, Mich.: Eerdmans, 1977] 16).

a. If the question is meant to stress a "clear claim," we can answer it in two ways: (i) If the historical Jesus ever explicitly claimed to be God, the Gospels have not so presented that claim. They never put on his lips *egō eimi theos,* "I am God." True, New Testament writers attribute the title *theos* to him (John 1:1; 20:28; Heb 1:8). However, this is a "confessional" title, i.e., one that manifests a certain belief in him and obviously corresponds to the period and experience of the Christianity which the writer represents. It is not a title that can with any certainty be attributed to his earthly ministry. When it emerges in the New Testament tradition, it is found in the later books.

(ii) If the words "clearly claimed" could be understood of an implication or impression conveyed by Jesus that he was a being who enjoyed a unique relationship to Yahweh or an "otherness" not shared by other heaven-sent emissaries, then one could give a guarded affirmative answer to the question. Various elements in the Synoptic and Johannine traditions about him (see §4d above) convey the notion that what he passed on to others was at most an implicit and indirect impression of that relationship. It took time for the explication and unfolding of that relationship which eventually was formulated in the New Testament itself: "and the Word was God" (John 1:1).

b. Two other comments must be made in this regard. (i) One of the religious charges leveled against Jesus by his contemporaries and reflected in various ways in the New Testament is that of "blasphemy" (Mark 2:7; 14:64; John 10:33,36). This undoubtedly echoes an early Christian recollection of the main charge brought against him, even though the diversity of the contexts in which it now appears makes it almost impossible for us to specify the particulars of that charge any further. However, it is not unlikely that it was associated with an impression that he had given about some unique relationship to Yahweh, that he was somehow on a par with Yahweh (see John 5:18). (ii) Would it have been possible in the monotheistic setting of pre-Christian Palestine for a Jew like Jesus to claim openly, *ănāh 'ĕlāhā'* (in Aramaic) or *egō eimi theos* (in Greek), "I am God"? Indeed, to ask the question is to answer it. It is impossible to imagine how such a statement would have been understood—given the fact that in most instances in the New Testament *theos* is the title used of Yahweh (of the one whom Jesus called *abba*). (See further §19 below.)

18.   What Is To Be Said of the Titles, Messiah or Christ, Son of Man, Son of God, Lord, etc.

Such titles are important data in the New Testament for its explicit christological teaching about Jesus and his role in the divine plan of salvation. For the most part, they are titles born of Christian (post-resurrectional) faith and represent confessional affirmations about him. Early Christians clearly used them, but the problem is to explain their emergence. Three questions have to be asked about them: (a) What is the origin or background of the title? (b) What did it mean? (c) To what phase of Jesus' existence was it initially applied? For some of them have been retrojected by hindsight into stories of the ministry or infancy from post-resurrection settings. Here it is impossible to discuss each of these aspects of the titles at length, but some brief remarks on each will be attempted.

With the possible exception of "Son of Man," there is no evidence that the earthly Jesus ever used these titles of himself.

a. "Messiah" (or "Christ") is a title derived from the Old Testament and from pre-Christian Palestinian Judaism. It designates an anointed agent sent by God for the welfare or salvation of his people. Used in the Old Testament for historical kings who sat on David's throne, it assumed political connotations (see Ps 18:51; 89:39,52; 132:10,17), assuring the continuance of the Davidic dynasty. In the exilic and post-exilic period, when the dynasty was no more, the title was used of the high priest (Lev 4:3,5). When the messianic expectation clearly emerged in Judaism, the first mention of a *coming* Messiah is found in Dan 9:25. About the same time the Qumran community begins to speak of a "Messiah of Israel" and a "Messiah of Aaron" (1QS 9:11), and begins to predicate the title even of Israel's prophets.

As a title for Jesus in the New Testament, it is missing in the "Q" source of the Synoptic tradition. In three places in the Marcan Gospel it probably reflects the post-resurrectional concerns of the early Christian Church (9:41; 13:21; 15:32). Whether three other Marcan passages that use it (8:29; 12:35; 14:61–62) are reflections of authentic usage is hotly debated.

In the first of these, Mark 8:29, Peter's confession of Jesus as "the Christ" (or "Messiah") forms the literary turning-point of Jesus' relation to his disciples and of the Marcan revelation of who Jesus is. Does it permit an historical deduction about Peter's recognition of Jesus during his ministry? I think that it enshrines something of a Petrine recognition, which may have been sharpened in time in its messianic form (recall the form the confession takes in the Johannine tradition of John 6:67–69). In favor of an affirmative deduction of some sort is the obvious rebuke of Peter by Jesus (modified in Matt 16:17–19 and mollified in Luke 9:20–22). Yet if Peter did historically admit that Jesus was the "Messiah" at Caesarea Philippi, one has to grant that the implication of that title was not yet what it became for post-resurrection Christianity. The rebuke at least meant the rejection of the political overtones associated with the title. (See §9 above.)

Again, in Mark 14:62, in the course of the interrogation before the Sanhedrin, Jesus is depicted giving an affirmative answer to the high priest's question, "Are you the Messiah?" But that frank affirmative Marcan answer has a parallel in Matt 26:64 and Luke 22:67–70 which is either only a half-affirmative answer or a non-committal response. Not only do the parallels raise a real question about the form of the historic answer, but this part of the passion narrative is not without its Marcan editorial concerns and redaction. It gives little basis for a judgment about Jesus' own messianic consciousness.

By the time that Paul wrote, "Christ" had already become a proper name, save in Rom 9:5. This Pauline use shows that this title was the most primitive and the most frequently used. It was most likely Pilate's inscription on the cross, "The King of the Jews" (Mark 15:26—note the slightly different wording of this *titulus* in the other Gospels, Matt 27:37; Luke 23:38; John 19:19) which served as the catalyst for the use of "Messiah" for a crucified anointed agent of Yahweh. The pre-Lucan (and most likely pre-Pauline) tradition embedded in Acts 2:36 suggests that Jesus was so hailed after the resurrection: "This Jesus whom you crucified . . . God has made both Lord and Messiah."

Still another early Christian understanding of his messiahship, however, is found in Acts 3:20–22, where God is said to be expected to send "the Messiah designated for you, Jesus, whom heaven must welcome until the time for establishing all that God has spoken about by the mouth of his holy prophets of old." This has been called the oldest christology preserved in the New Testament, relating Jesus' messiahship not to his resurrection, but to his parousia. Here he would be still expected to come as "Messiah." This is not impossible. It would give a clearer understanding to the process of retrojection of titles from a later phase of Christ's existence to an earlier, which seems at times to have been at work. On the other hand, it may also be a remnant of a parakerygmatic christology, a belief in the parousiac Jesus as Messiah, which had some vogue in a part of the early Christian Church, but which never caught on or became as influential as the kerygmatic proclamation of him as Messiah as of the resurrection. These are reflections of different ways in which early Christians understood Jesus' messiahship and which point *mainly* to a post-resurrection emergence of the title. (See further §9 above.)

b. The titles "Son of God" and "Lord" are not only of Palestinian Jewish origin, but are also clear examples of confessional titles used of Jesus which emerged in the post-resurrectional period. Even though *divi filius,* "son of God," and *kyrios,* "lord," were titles current in the Greco-Roman world of the time, used of the Roman emperor and/or pagan deities, and may be reflected in such New Testament passages as 1 Cor 8:5 or Acts 25:26, this evidence cannot be claimed as the sole origin of the titles "Son of God" or "Lord" for Jesus in the New Testament writings.

c. There is now evidence to show that "Son of God" was used in Palestinian Judaism in pre-Christian times by Aramaic speakers and that the absolute use of "(the) Lord" was also attributed to Yahweh himself (see my article, "The Contribution of Qumran Aramaic to the Study of the New Testament," *NTS* 20 [1973–74] 382–407, esp. pp. 386–94; reprinted in *A Wandering Aramean: Collected Aramaic Essays* [SBLMS 25; Missoula, Mt.: Scholars, 1979] 85–113, esp. pp. 87–94; cf. M. Hengel, *The Son of God* [Philadelphia: Fortress, 1976]). These, then, are titles which must have quickly emerged as the kerygma was formulated; they are not solely the product of missionary endeavor, as that kerygma was carried from Palestine to the eastern Mediterranean Greco-Roman world, as has often been maintained. When these post-resurrectional titles appear earlier in the Gospel tradition (e.g., Matt 16:16b; Luke 1:32,35; 2:11; 12:42), they are to be regarded as retrojections of the evangelists who used of the earthly Jesus titles current for him in the post-resurrection period or in their own day (see the discussion on "Son of the living God" in §9g above).

d. The greatest debate at present surrounds the title "Son of Man." In the vast majority of instances it is found on the lips of Jesus himself; but it is used of him by others in Acts 7:56 (Stephen); John 12:34 (the crowd); and Mark 2:10 and par. (the evangelist[s], even though in this case many commentators use subterfuges, such as anacoluthon, to claim that this instance too appears on his lips). Because "Son of Man" does so appear in many cases, the question arises whether Jesus actually used the term *bar 'enās* or *bar 'enāsā'* in his ministry to refer indirectly to himself. This is a legitimate question, even if one has to realize that the title has been secondarily introduced into certain passages by an evangelist, where the parallel passage lacks it (cf. Mark 8:27c ["Who do people say that I am?"] and Matt 16:13 ["Who do people say that the Son of Man is?"]; similarly Luke 6:22 and Matt 5:11).

"Son of Man" is found in both the Johannine and the Synoptic traditions (with different nuances, to be sure) and it does not purport to be a confessional title. It plays no role in the christology of other New Testament writings, save in the Book of Revelation. The awkward Greek phrase *ho huios tou anthrōpou* (literally, "the son of the man") scarcely permits one to derive this title from a Hellenistic background. Because it sometimes occurs without the definite articles (*huios anthrōpou* [e.g., John 5:27]) and resembles a Semitic construct-chain, it is usually regarded as a translation of *bar 'enās(ā')*. But its denotation is highly disputed.

Was it a title for an expected apocalyptic figure in pre-Christian Palestinian Judaism? A mere development from a non-titular synonym (= "human being" [generically] or "someone" [indefinitely]) or from a substitute-expression for "I" or "he"? There is no evidence in Aramaic for the use of "Son of Man" as a title for an individual expected or apocalyptic figure; in Dan 7:13 the phrase occurs, but it is designation for the corporate "saints" of Israel. The titular use of the phrase in Enochic literature is likewise highly contested. The substitution of "Son of Man" for "I" in some New Testament passages (see above) has raised the question about the phrase as a substitute-expression. This use is found in some Aramaic writings of later centuries (scarcely before A.D. 300), but has as yet not been found in any contemporary Aramaic texts. In my opinion, the titular use of the phrase for Jesus in the New Testament is best explained as a development in the early Christian community from sayings in which he used the phrase "Son of Man" of himself in a non-titular and non-substitute sense, meaning nothing more than "a human being." In the pre-written Gospel tradition it then assumed a titular sense, and that is why it was preserved in its barbarous Greek form. The connotations which the phrase carries in various New Testament contexts, however, have to be scrutinized individually.

Finally, the title is applied to Jesus in the Synoptics in three main ways: (i) it is used of Jesus in his lowly, earthly condition (Matt 8:20; Luke 9:58); (ii) it is used of him in reference to his passion (lacking in "Q," but see Mark 8:31; 9:31; 10:33); and (iii) it is used of him coming in glory or judgment ("Q": Matt 24:27; Luke 17:24; and Mark 8:38; 13:26). Though each of these three senses is transmitted in the Gospel tradition, it is not possible to establish any real connection among them. In my opinion, it is highly unlikely that Jesus himself ever used the phrase as a title of some expected figure apart from himself (for the reason stated above).

19. After the Resurrection Was Jesus Proclaimed Unambiguously from the Start as Son of God, Equal to the Father?

a. The earliest use of "Son" for Jesus in the New Testament is found in what is usually regarded as a pre-Pauline kerygmatic fragment in Paul's first letter, 1 Thess 1:10: "to wait for his Son from

heaven, whom he raised from the dead, Jesus who delivers us from
the wrath to come." In a similar fragment (Rom 1:3–4) there is a
double use of "Son": the first may be Pauline and refer to Jesus as
pre-existent, whereas the second, the pre-Pauline usage, speaks of his
being constituted or appointed "Son of God in power" as of the resurrection from the dead. Elsewhere in Paul's writings we find reference to Jesus as God's "Son" (e.g., Gal 1:16; 4:4–6; 1 Cor 15:28;
Rom 8:32). In later New Testament writings this title continues in
use. The Pauline references, however, show that it did not take long
for Christians to recognize Jesus' relationship to Yahweh precisely
under this title. M. Hengel (in the book cited in §18c above) argues
strongly that this belief emerged between A.D. 30 and 50.

b. Was the title used of him "unambiguously from the start"?
This is not easy to say. Even those New Testament interpreters who
would regard some of the early speeches in Acts as reflecting the
primitive kerygma—a view that is not universally admitted—would
have to agree that "Son" is hardly a title associated with this form of
the kerygma. The early chapters of Acts use many titles of Jesus (see
§12c above), some of which are pre-Lucan, but "Son" appears only
in Paul's preaching (Acts 9:20 and 13:33 [the latter in a quotation
from Ps 2:7, applied to the risen Christ]).

c. Even if one asserts that "Son" was a title used very early of
Jesus, it is not easy to say that it meant "equal to the Father." Of
itself, it implies subordination, that of a natural son to his father. Jesus, however, was not *abba,* and in its confession of Jesus, the New
Testament never identifies him with the Father (see §17 above). (He
is one with the Father in the Johannine claim of 10:30.) 1 Cor 15:25–
28 speaks openly of his subjection even as "the Son himself" (cf. Heb
1:2–8). On the other hand, in giving him the title *kyrios,* a title used
of Yahweh in Palestinian Judaism (see Ps 114:7; 11QtgJob24:7;
1QapGen 20:12–13, 4QEnoch[b] 1 iv 5; Josephus, *Ant.* 20.4,2 §90;
13.3,1 §68), it implied that he was somehow on a level with Yahweh,
without, however, being identified with him or made absolutely
equal to him (*Gleichsetzung, nicht Identifizierung!*).

d. The phrase "equality with God" is used of Jesus in the pre-Pauline hymn in Phil 2:6. But it is quite disputed in what sense that phrase is to be understood: whether that equality was something that was his and that he did not hesitate to give up (in his *kenōsis*), or was something that he did not have and did not even grasp after. Yet even so, it is precisely these ambiguous New Testament phrases which led in time to the clearer reconceptualization and reformulation of the relationship of him to God which we know about from later christological and trinitarian teaching of the patristic period. If it were not for this ambiguity of the New Testament usage, how would Christians ever have come to the idea of three distinct persons in the Trinity? On the other hand, that same hymn clearly states that God gave him a name which was above every other name (viz., *kyrios,* "Lord") and that he was accorded the adoration of every knee in creation (using a phrase which speaks of the same kind of adoration of Yahweh, in Isa 45:23).

e. The notion of Jesus as "Son" is also found in the Johannine tradition. It is almost certainly not to be regarded solely as the addition of the final redactor(s) of the Fourth Gospel. There is, however, a peculiarly Johannine cast to the use of "Son" in this Gospel which prevents one from predicating this usage of Christian belief "from the start." Even though the assertion of Jesus' oneness with the Father is expressed in various ways (10:30,38; 17:21), it has to be understood primarily of a functional christology (i.e., of a belief in the *meaning* of Christ *for* human beings). Yet the Christian reflection and meditation present in this Gospel are likewise a prime factor in the development of explicit ontological christology (i.e., a belief in the intrinsic constitution of Christ and of his relation to the Father) of a later date.

20. How Does Contemporary New Testament Scholarship Understand the Claim that Jesus of Nazareth Was the Redeemer of the World?

From the standpoint of New Testament interpretation the question could be understood in two ways.

a. It could refer to the cosmic dimension of redemption. In the New Testament *kosmos* can denote the world as the "ordered universe" (John 17:5; Luke 11:50; Acts 17:24; 1 Cor 8:4). Paul sees the effects of the Christ-event spilling over and influencing not only human beings, but even material or physical creation in general. In Rom 11:15 he speaks of the "reconciliation of the world" (a slogan not further explained in this passage, in which he is treating of Israel's place or relation to the divine plan of salvation). He may be echoing there 2 Cor 5:19, where he said that "God was in Christ reconciling the world to himself." In both of these passages Paul seems to view the Christ-event as having an effect not only on human beings but on the created universe itself. Compare what he says about the "eager longing" of material "creation" *(ktisis)* and its relation to the inward groaning of Christians awaiting the "redemption of their bodies" (Rom 8:19–23). Though it is not easy to explain further this cosmic dimension of redemption, Paul's words have a peculiar ring today, when we hear so much about ecology and reflect on what human beings in their greed, lack of concern for others, and profligacy have been doing to God's good earth. Environmental control is something that has been born of modern industrial and technological society, but perhaps Paul even saw the analogous need of something similar in the world in which he lived, devoid of such effects of so-called modern progress.

b. The question could refer to the universe of human beings or to the application of the effects of the Christ-event to *all* mankind. Paul, for instance, indicts all humanity: "Since all have sinned and fall short of the glory of God, they are justified by his grace as a gift, through the redemption which is in Christ Jesus" (Rom 3:23–24). In that context Paul was thinking of Jews and Greeks without the Gospel: "All human beings, both Jews and Greeks, are under the power of sin" (3:9). Taking a cue from other New Testament passages, such as 1 Tim 2:4–5 (God "desires all human beings to be saved and to come to the knowledge of the truth; for there is one God and one mediator between God and men, the man Christ Jesus, who gave himself as a ransom for all"), Christian theologians have easily and rightly concluded to the role of Jesus as the redeemer of the world, i.e., of the universe of human beings. This is at least the thrust of much New Testament data that bear on this topic; recall the "universalism" of salvation in Lucan writings or the Johannine stress on the salvation of the world (4:42; 12:47).

c. What bearing does the New Testament material have on the salvation of peoples of other cultures not specifically influenced by Christianity? That question is more properly addressed to a systematic theologian, because it is not within the purview of the New Testament writings. Even the "other sheep who are not of this fold" (John 10:16) cannot be extended to all non-Christians without further ado, since there is some likelihood that within the Johannine writings that verse refers to other Christians who were not accepting the Johannine view of the Christ-event with its "high" christology and "closed" ecclesiology. (See further R. E. Brown, *The Community of the Beloved Disciple* [see §6d above].)

d. A specifically acute problem that Christian theologians have to work out better in this regard is the salvation of the Jews. For Christian thinkers have not really developed a satisfactory "theology of Israel." The problem is to explain how a group of people, feeding and nourishing its religious life on two-thirds of what Christians call the Bible, yet not accepting the last third of it and him whom it proclaims, can continue to find its salvation by following the law of Moses, the prophets, and the writings, without accepting him whom Christians call "the redeemer of the world." The problem itself was given a bit of treatment in Romans 9–11, at a very early stage of Christian thinking, but that is scarcely an answer to the existence of Judaism parallel to Christianity in God's plan of salvation for almost nineteen centuries.

APPENDIX

1.

The Biblical Commission and Its Instruction on the Historical Truth of the Gospels

The Biblical Commission

In 1902, by his Apostolic Letter *Vigilantiae*[1] Pope Leo XIII established the Pontifical Biblical Commission.

At that time Leo XIII gave the Commission the twofold task of *promoting* biblical interpretation in agreement with his encyclical *Providentissimus Deus*[2] and of *guarding* the Bible against false interpretations. His Apostolic Letter began with the word "Vigilantiae" (Watchfulness, Vigilance), and the watchdog aspect of the Commission prevailed, reflecting the troubled period in which it was set up. Though the Biblical Commission was not a Roman congregation in the strict sense, it was organized like one of the curial congregations (with cardinal members and consultors).

Under Pope Pius X its task was determined anew. The Commission was to exercise its watchfulness by answering questions from Catholics about biblical problems. This it did above all by *responsa,* the technical term for its more-popularly called Decrees. These decrees were usually stylized in the form of questions—often loaded— to which a brief answer (*responsum)* was given, either *negative* or *affirmative.* The series of fourteen *responsa* issued between 1905 and 1915 became the hallmark of the Commission. They treated such matters as the following: the theory of implicit quotations; the theory of apparently historical narratives; the Mosaic authorship of the Pen-

---

1. *ASS* 35 (1902–3) 234–38; *EnchBib* §137–38; cf. A. Kleinhans, *LTK* 2. 359–60.

2. *ASS* 26 (1893–94) 269–92; *EnchBib* §81–134; DS §3280–94.

tateuch; the author and historical reliability of the Fourth Gospel; Isaiah; the historicity of Genesis 1–3; the author and date of the Psalms; Matthew, Mark, and Luke; the Synoptic problem; Acts; the Pastoral Letters; the Epistle to the Hebrews; the parousia in Pauline writings.[3] As a result of these *responsa* a dark cloud of reactionary conservatism settled over Roman Catholic biblical scholarship during the first half of the twentieth century.

The decrees of the Biblical Commission were not infallibly issued. Pius X explained that they were "useful for the proper progress and the guidance of biblical scholarship along safe paths" and required of Catholics the same submission as similar papally approved decrees of other Roman congregations.[4] Thus was formulated their utilitarian and practical aim.

In the midst of World War II Pope Pius XII issued an encyclical on the promotion of biblical studies, *Divino afflante Spiritu* (1943).[5] Since that time the Biblical Commission began to play a more open-minded role in promoting Catholic biblical scholarship. Its *responsa* gradually gave way to "letters" and "instructions," which, though they sometimes expressed cautions about popular errors or excessive tendencies, gradually assumed a more positive char-

---

3. These and other early utterances can be found in *EnchBib* §160–61, 181–84, 187–89, 276–80, 324–31, 332–39, 383–89, 390–400, 401–6, 407–10, 411–13, 414–16; *RSS,* 117–38. For a modern commentary on these *responsa* see T. A. Collins and R. E. Brown, "Church Pronouncements," *JBC,* art. 72, §25–28. For a few later utterances of the Commission, less pertinent to the topic under discussion here, see *EnchBib* §522–33, 535–37, 582–610, 622–33; *RSS,* 138–49, 154–72; cf. *JBC,* art. 72, 29–30, 32–33.

4. Motuproprio *Praestantia sacrae Scripturae* (*ASS* 40 [1907] 723–26; *EnchBib* §268–73; DS §3503; *RSS,* 40–42): ". . . all are obliged in conscience *to submit* to past and future decisions of the Biblical Commission *in the same way as to the decrees which pertain to doctrine issued by* [*other*] *sacred congregations and approved by the Pope"* (§271). This clarification was repeated in a *responsum* of the Commission itself issued on 27 February 1934 (*AAS* 26 [1934] 130–31; *EnchBib* §519). There ensued a discussion among theologians of the time about the character of the responses of the Commission, whether they were disciplinary or doctrinal. The majority of them seem to have thought that they were not merely disciplinary, but "indirectly doctrinal."

acter. The changed image became apparent in January 1948, when the Commission issued a nuanced answer to a (real) question addressed to it by Cardinal Suhard of Paris about the character of the first eleven chapters of Genesis.[6] In 1951, when the Commission revised the list of topics for examinations to be taken to obtain ecclesiastical biblical degrees, it significantly dropped its own (formerly required) decrees.[7]

To many, both inside and outside the Catholic Church, however, the decrees seemed to be still in effect and the Commission seemed to be still the vigilance committee of old. In 1955 a semi-official explanation of the character of the decrees was issued. The secretary of the Commission, A. Miller. O.S.B., reviewed in *Benediktinische Monatsschrift* a newly revised edition of *Enchiridion biblicum,* a collection of Church documents concerning biblical interpretation which were published across the centuries.[8] At the same time, the subsecretary of the Commission, A. Kleinhans, O.F.M., did the same in the Roman periodical *Antonianum.*[9] Both reviewers, though they wrote in different languages (the former in German, the latter in Latin), significantly used in paragraphs of identical wording an important distinction about the decrees. They distinguished the decrees which touched upon faith and morals from those which dealt with literary criticism, authorship, integrity, date of composition, and similar questions. The former were to be understood as still valid; the latter were to be regarded as time-conditioned and corresponding to an historical context no longer existent. The two secretaries of the Commission frankly stated that Catholic scholars

---

There was also a discussion whether they were concerned with *veritas* (truth) or *securitas* (security). See L. Pirot, "Commission biblique," *DBS* 2. 111–13.

5. *AAS* 35 (1943) 297–326; *EnchBib* §538–69; DS §3825–31; cf. *JBC,* art. 72, §20–23.

6. *AAS* 40 (1948) 45–48; *EnchBib* §577–81; *RSS,* 150–53; cf. *JBC,* art. 72, §31.

7. *AAS* 43 (1951) 748; *EnchBib* §638. Compare *AAS* 3 (1911) 48.

8. "Das neue biblische Handbuch," *BenMon* 31 (1955) 49–50.

9. "De nova Enchiridii biblici editione," *Anton* 30 (1955) 53–65.

could in matters related to the latter group of decrees pursue their investigations, research, and interpretation "with full freedom" (in *aller Freiheit, plena libertate*). The significance of this distinction was not lost on Roman Catholic interpreters and was even brought to the attention of Protestant scholars.[10]

As a matter of fact, almost all the decrees of the Biblical Commission issued between 1905 and 1915, at the height of the reaction to modernism, belong to the second category. Say what one will about the character of the distinction made by the two secretaries of the Commission, the advances made by Catholic biblical scholars in

---

10. See E. F. Siegman, "The Decrees of the Pontifical Biblical Commission: A Recent Clarification," *CBQ* 18 (1956) 23–29. For a different view of the distinction made by the secretaries of the Commission, see J. E. Steinmueller, *A Companion to Scripture Studies* (3 vols.; rev. ed.; New York: Wagner, 1969) 1. 301; he accuses Siegman of having "falsely concluded that the decrees have been tacitly revoked and are now only of historical interest." He goes even further in a more recent publication (*The Sword of the Spirit* [Waco, Tex.: Stella Maris Books, 1977] 7 n. 1) in maintaining that the articles of Miller and Kleinhans were *unauthorized* and the two secretaries were to be brought before the Holy Office because of these articles but were saved from this ordeal through the personal intervention of Cardinal Tisserant before the Holy Father. This is the recollection of an old conservative, first published twenty-two years after the fact; why did this allegation not emerge sooner? The point is that, as Steinmueller reveals, the secretaries were *not* brought before the Holy Office; such a political move was thwarted. This can scarcely be regarded as "the real explanation," *pace* J. P. O'Reilly (*The Priest* 36 [1980] 6). Here the principle, *tacere est consentire,* is valid; failure to speak against the secretaries equals consent to their affirmations.

That Siegman's interpretation of the clarification is correct may be shown in various ways. A very similar interpretation was given in Europe by J. Dupont, O.S.B., "A propos du nouvel Enchiridion biblicum," *RB* 62 (1955) 414–19. Moreover, many Roman Catholic interpreters of no little stature have been acting in their study and research on such an interpretation; and not a few of them have subsequently been named either consultors or members of the Biblical Commission itself. Such a respected French Dominican Old Testament scholar as A. M. Dubarle had even managed to publish a letter about the matter, prior to this semi-official clarification, in the leading German Protestant biblical periodical in order to offset the views of outsiders about the freedom of Catholic exegetes; see "Lettre à la rédaction," *ZAW* 66 (1954) 149–51.

The reader should beware of the summary of the clarification given in *RSS,* 175–76, which omits all reference to the crucial phrases, *in aller Freiheit, plena libertate,* "with all freedom."

the last twenty-five years and the acceptance of their work in non-Roman Catholic circles reveal the validity and significance of that distinction.

Since the encyclical *Divino afflante Spiritu* and the letter sent to Cardinal Suhard the Biblical Commission has issued an instruction about the treatment of biblical subjects in seminaries and houses of theological study of religious orders and congregations (1950)[11] and a Declaration (1953) about a book on the Psalms.[12]

In June 1961 a Roman *monitum* was issued concerning the historicity of the Bible.[13] Significantly enough, it came not from the Biblical Commission, but from the Holy Office (as the Congregation for the Doctrine of the Faith was then called). An appended brief note recorded that the agreement of the cardinals of the Biblical Commission had been obtained for the *monitum*. Nevertheless, it was clear that the watchdog role was now being played by a different Roman congregation.

By this time the Biblical Commission itself had gone through a process of opening up, leading to the positive promotion of biblical

---

11. *AAS* 42 (1950) 495–505, *EnchBib* §582–610; *RSS*, 134–67.

12. *AAS* 45 (1953) 432; *EnchBib* §621.

13. *AAS* 53 (1961) 507; *RSS*, 174 (the reader should again beware of the tendentious title put on the translation here; the *monitum* was not addressed solely to "Biblical Scholars").

The text of the *monitum* reads:

Suprema S. Congregatio S. Officii
Biblicarum disciplinarum studio laudabiliter fervente, in variis regionibus sententiae et opiniones circumferuntur, quae in discrimen adducunt germanam veritatem historicam et obiectivam Scripturae Sacrae non modo Veteris Testamenti (sicut Summus Pontifex Pius XII in Litteris Encyclicis "Human Generis" iam deploraverat, cfr. *A. A. S.* XLII, 576) verum et Novi, etiam quoad dicta et facta Christi Iesu.

Though biblical studies are progressing in a praiseworthy manner, assertions and opinions are circulating here and there which call in question the proper historical and objective truth of Sacred Scripture—not only of the Old Testament (as Pope Pius XII had already sadly noted in his encyclical "Humani Generis" [cf. *AAS* 42 (1950) 576]) but also of the New, even with regard to the words and deeds of Christ Jesus.

studies. In 1963 five distinguished European biblical scholars, noted for their openness to modern interpretation of the Bible, were associated with the Commission as consultors: R. Schnackenburg (Germany), C. Spicq, O.P. (Switzerland), X. Léon-Dufour, S.J. (France), B. Rigaux, O.F.M. (Belgium), and G. Castellino, S.D.B. (Italy). This list of consultors was further expanded in 1965 by other well-known and respected names of contemporary scholarship: B. M. Ahern, C.P. (United States), R. A. F. MacKenzie, S.J. (Canada), P. W. Skehan (United States), H. Schürmann (East Germany), R. Lach (France), and G. Rinaldi (Italy). In 1964 three new cardinals were added to the Commission, two of whom were biblical specialists: B. Alfrink (Holland), F. König (Austria), and I. Antoniutti (Italy). True, the conservative Cardinals A. Ottaviani, E. Ruffini, and M. Browne, O.P. were still retained as members of the Commission, but their influence was now counterbalanced. The image of the Commission itself was gradually changing.

Cum autem huiusmodi sententiae et opiniones anxios faciant et Pastores et christifideles, Em.mi Patres, fidei morumque doctrinae tutandae praepositi, omnes qui de Sacris Libris sive scripto sive verbo agunt, monendos censuerunt ut semper debita cum prudentia ac reverentia tantum argumentum pertractent, et prae oculis semper habeant SS. Patrum doctrinam atque Ecclesiae sensum ac Magisterium, ne fidelium conscientiae perturbentur neve fidei veritates laedatur.	Since such assertions and opinions create anxieties for both pastors and the faithful, the cardinals who are charged with the protection of doctrine on faith and morals have considered it necessary to warn all those who deal with the sacred writings either orally or in writing to treat so great a subject with prudence and reverence. Let them always pay attention to the teaching of the Fathers, the mind of the Church, and the magisterium, lest consciences be disturbed or truths of the faith be harmed.
N.B.—Hoc Monitum editur consentientibus etiam Em.mis Patribus Pontificiae Commissionis Biblicae.	This warning is issued with the agreement of the Cardinals of the Pontifical Biblical Commission.

Cf. *TS* 22 (1961) 442–44 for an explanation of *germanam veritatem historicam et obiectivam.*

A further step in the change of the image of the Commission was taken in its Instruction of 1964 on the historical truth of the Gospels. This Instruction showed that the Commission could concretely handle in a positive way a problem which vexed many modern Christian students of the Bible both in and outside of the Roman communion. In that Instruction a distinction was proposed which is fundamental for the proper interpretation of the canonical Gospels by anyone who would try to understand what they are all about.

Before turning to that Instruction, however, we should add two further developments of later date to complete this brief sketch of the role of the Biblical Commission in the modern Roman Catholic Church and of the transformed image projected by it in the last decade and a half. *First,* the fundamental distinction proposed by the Commission in its Instruction of 1964 was adopted by the fathers of Vatican Council II in chapter 5 of the Apostolic Constitution *Dei Verbum,* which treated of the New Testament and its relation to revelation.[14] Thus the authority of an ecumenical council was added to the proposal made in the 1964 Instruction of the Biblical Commission. *Second,* in 1971 Pope Paul VI completely revamped the Biblical Commission, making it a counterpart of the Theological Commission, associating both of them more closely to the Congregation of the Doctrine of the Faith, and staffing it no longer with cardinals but with twenty members of international background—many of them biblical scholars of recognized competence.[15]

---

14. *Dei verbum* §19; *AAS* 58 (1966) 817–36, esp. pp. 826–27. See pp. 141–42 below.

15. Motuproprio *Sedula cura* (*AAS* 63 [1971] 665–69). In its newly constituted form the Biblical Commission has issued no document so far, but only a collection of essays (see p. 143). One report prepared by it on the New Testament data about the possible ordination of women was leaked to the press; see "Can Women Be Priests?" *Origins* 6 (1976–77) 92–96. Cf. the Sacred Congregation for the Doctrine of the Faith, "Declaration on the Question of the Admission of Women to the Ministerial Priesthood," ibid., 517–24. The names of the present members of the Commission can be found in *Annuario pontificio 1981,* 1091.

The Instruction of 1964

The Instruction *Sancta Mater Ecclesia* dealt with "the historical truth of the Gospels."[16] It treated of a problem that had been the concern of many Catholics in the immediately preceding decades, which surfaced in the discussions of the bishops at the beginning of Vatican Council II, and which continues to be of concern to many theologians and lay people. Unfortunately, the sage advice which was incorporated in the Instruction has frequently been ignored in the circles where it is needed most.

That an age-old problem has been posed in a new way was evident from the *monitum* of 1961, published by the Holy Office on the same subject.[17] That document, however, was wholly negative in character and shed no light on the problem itself. The Instruction of the Biblical Commission, coming at a time when it did—during the course of Vatican Council II—proved to be, by contrast, a positive document of no little importance. Given the trend of modern Catholic Gospel studies in the immediately preceding decade and the diverse reaction to them in the Church at large, there is reason to study the Instruction in some detail to appreciate its importance.

---

16. The first publication of "Instructio de historica evangeliorum veritate" appeared in *OssRom* 14 May 1964, p. 3 (with an accompanying Italian translation); the definitive publication is found in *AAS* 56 (1964) 712–18. Cf. DS §3999-99e.

An English translation of the Instruction appeared in Catholic newspapers in the United States; because it was faulty in places and unreliable in crucial paragraphs, I appended to the original form of this discussion an improved translation prepared from the Latin text in *OssRom*. This translation, now slightly revised, follows the present commentary. My translation preserves the paragraphing of the original. Only certain paragraphs in the Latin text are numbered with arabic numerals; they have been retained. To facilitate reference to the text of the Instruction, however, I have added roman numerals to all of its paragraphs in my translation.

After this translation and commentary were prepared, the secretary of the Biblical Commission sent out an English version of the Instruction. It can be found in *CBQ* 26 (1964) 305–12; *Tablet* (London) 218 (30 May 1964) 617–19; *TBT* 13 (1964) 821–28; *AER* 151 (1964) 5–11.

17. See n. 13 above.

That the Instruction was a well-nuanced document became evident from newspaper reports announcing its publication; some of the best of them interpreted it in almost diametrically opposed senses. The *New York Times* ran a headline: "Vatican Cautions Students of the Bible; Rejects as Dangerous and Invalid Any Conclusions Not Arising from Faith; Inquiry Limits Defined; Modern Historical Methods Accepted If Scholars Are Wary of 'Prejudices.' "[18] On the contrary, the *New York Herald Tribune* summed up its report under the headline: "Vatican Gives Green Light to Biblical Scholars."[19]

When studied closely, however, the Instruction was seen to be a document which does not commit Catholic students of the Gospels to a fundamentalistic literalness in the matter of their historicity. It contains no condemnation of any specific modern opinion about the historical value of the Gospels. Though it catalogues in some detail questionable presuppositions of many form critics, this is done to clear the way to a recognition of the permanent value of the form-critical method itself. Consequently, the Instruction is an historic "first"—the first official ecclesiastical statement openly countenancing biblical criticism and frankly admitting the distinction of three stages of the Gospel tradition which has emerged from the form-critical study of the Gospels.

The Title of the Instruction

The 1964 document is entitled *Instructio de historica evangeliorum veritate* ("An Instruction about the Historical Truth of the Gospels"). A close analysis of its text reveals that the most important word in the title is not the adjective *historica*—which might have

---

18. *The New York Times,* 14 May 1964, 37 (article written by R. C. Doty). His inaccurate summary of the Instruction was irresponsibly reproduced in great part in *HPR* 64 (1963–64) 773 ("Attention Biblical Scholars").

19. *New York Herald Tribune,* 14 May 1964, 7 (article written by S. de Gramont).

been one's initial expectation—but the preposition *de* ("about"). Significantly, par. III,[20] which states the problem, omits the word "historical": "because many writings are being spread abroad in which the truth of the deeds and words which are contained in the Gospels is questioned."[21] In the light of the rest of the Instruction the omission of the adjective seems intentional. In fact, though *historica veritas* appears in the title of the document, it is used only once in its text, and then in a sentence in which is decried a certain philosophical or theological presupposition of the form-critical method, to which no Catholic exegete would subscribe anyway.[22] In none of the positive directives of the Instruction does the phrase "historical truth" reappear. The Biblical Commission was evidently far more interested in sketching in broad lines the *character* of the truth of the Gospels than in just reasserting that the Gospels are "historical."

The Structure of the Instruction

After three introductory paragraphs the Commission addresses directives to (a) exegetes, (b) professors of Scripture in seminaries and similar institutions, (c) preachers, (d) those who publish for the faithful, and (e) directors of biblical associations. Under (d) ordinaries (i.e., above all the diocesan bishops) are reminded to be vigilant of publications on Scripture. Except for the first group (a)—and the

---

20. On the numbering of the paragraphs, see n. 16 above.

21. The Latin text runs: ". . . quod multa scripta vulgantur, quibus veritas factorum et dictorum quae in evangeliis continentur, in discrimen vocatur." This sentence echoes the wording of the *monitum* of the Holy Office. But it is noteworthy that a simpler phraseology has now been used. The *monitum* had complained of assertions and opinions which were circulating, "which call in question the proper historical and objective truth of Sacred Scripture, not only of the Old Testament . . . but also of the New, even with regard to the words and deeds of Christ Jesus" (see the Latin text in n. 13 above).

22. Par. V (middle). The Latin text reads, "Alii e falsa notione fidei procedunt ac si ipsa veritatem historicam non curet, immo cum eadem componi non possit."—The immediately following sentence uses the phrase "historicam vim et indolem documentorum revelationis," an expression which has a wider connotation.

omission may be a mere typographical error—the groups addressed are clearly mentioned in italics. In the directives addressed to the exegetes, italics are again used to indicate the three stages of the Gospel tradition discussed there. In this way the structure of the document is evident.[23] The conclusion consists of two paragraphs, in the last of which appears the approval of Pope Paul VI, dated 21 April 1964.

The Introduction (Paragraphs I–III)

The Church's concern for the Scriptures is recalled as the basis and background for all the work of the exegete. He is urged to rely not only on his resources, but also on God's help and the light of the Church.

In par. II joy is expressed at the growing number of competent interpreters of the Bible in the Church of today. Explicit recognition is made of the fact that they have been following papal encouragements. This clause was obviously incorporated into the Instruction in order to offset the criticism heard at times in Catholic circles that "exegetes" have been undermining the faith with their new interpretations. There follows a counsel to charity which is needed in this area so peculiarly prone to emotional discussion. It repeats the counsels found in *Divino afflante Spiritu* and *Vigilantiae*. Tucked away between the quotations is the remark that not even St. Jerome was always successful in handling the scriptural difficulties of his time.[24]

---

23. The italics of the original are preserved in my translation of the Instruction so that the structure of the document should be evident. The principle underlying the use of arabic numbers for certain paragraphs, however, changes after a while; though they too have been preserved, they are not a real guide to the structure. My references will always make use of the added roman numerals. On the opening sentence of the Instruction, see G. F. Woods, *TS* 27 (1966) 725.

24. For an example of the troubles which Jerome had, see my résumé of an episode in his life concerning the translation of Hebrew *qîqāyôn* of Jonah 4:6, *TS* 22 (1961) 426–27. He used "ivy" (*hedera*), whereas older Latin versions had "gourd" (*cucurbita*), and Augustine took him to task for it.

Paragraph III is like a topic sentence. It sets forth the problem to be discussed and states the Commission's purpose in issuing the Instruction.

Directives for Exegetes (Paragraphs IV–XI)

Eight of the following fifteen paragraphs of the Instruction are addressed to exegetes (pars. IV–XI). When these paragraphs are compared with the rest of the document, it is evident that its essential directives are found in this part. The directives for seminary professors, preachers, popular writers, and directors of biblical associations are hortatory and prudential. Exhortations and cautions are, of course, included in the directives to the exegetes; but it is only in this part of the Instruction that one finds directives of a positive, didactic nature.

Paragraph IV begins with an exhortation addressed to "Catholic exegetes" (*exegeta catholicus*). They are counseled to derive profit from *all* the contributions of former interpreters, especially from those of the Fathers and Doctors of the Church. In this, they are to follow the example of the Church itself. Moreover, they are also urged to utilize the norms of "rational" and "Catholic hermeneutics." What is meant here by "rational" hermeneutics is the universally admitted principles of criticism which prevail in the study of all forms of literature (in contrast to certain "fads" such as emerge from time to time). Such principles would include the norms of literary and historical criticism which guide any philologian or interpreter of ancient or modern literature or documents. The addition of "Catholic" defines further norms which must guide the Catholic interpreter (e.g., that the Bible is a collection of inspired writings, that genuine revelation is contained in them, that their fundamental purpose is the upbuilding of the people of God, etc.). What is especially meant by the norms of rational and Catholic hermeneutics is further explained by the recommendation of the aids offered by historical method. In particular, one is singled out from among them: The Commission urges the exegete once again to study the literary form used by the sacred writer. The Instruction recalls the words of Pius XII and stresses that the use of this mode of interpretation is his *duty* and that it may not be neglected.[25] Alas, this directive of the Instruction has not always been heeded in the time since its publication.

Particularly important is the following sentence of par. IV stating that a general rule of hermeneutics is applicable to both the Old and New Testaments: the composition of their books has been guided by modes of thinking and writing contemporary with their authors (and not necessarily with those of modern readers). This indirect reference to the nature of the Gospel testimony briefly outlines the bulk of the following directives in pars. VII–X. For the investigation of the modes of speech and of literary forms—in effect, what is usually referred to as form criticism—cannot be dispensed with in the interpretation of any biblical books, not even of the canonical Gospels. Thus, in the last sentences of par. IV are set forth the guiding principles of the whole Instruction. *First,* the interpreter must use "all the means available" in the interpretation of the Gospels; no method or means of interpretation may be excluded a priori, but all are to be used in an intelligent way to attain the goal intended.

---

25. An outspoken opponent of the study of the literary forms of the Bible was E. Cardinal Ruffini. He was a member of the Biblical Commission, at the time when this Instruction was issued, which publicly reiterated the injunction of Pius XII to the exegetes of the Church in *Divino afflante Spiritu* to pursue such study, especially with regard to the Gospels. Cardinal Ruffini's rejection of this type of interpretation can be found in his article, "Generi letterari e ipotesi di lavoro nei recenti studi biblici," *Oss-Rom* 24 August 1961, p. 1. Having appeared on the first page of such a prominent Church-organ and having been sent by the Sacred Congregation of Studies and Universities to the rectors of all Italian seminaries, it was accorded no little respect. It appeared in an English version in many Catholic newspapers in the United States; cf. "Literary Genres and Working Hypotheses in Recent Biblical Studies," *AER* 145 (1961) 362–65. In this article Cardinal Ruffini went so far in his disagreement as to quote Pius XII indirectly and to use the word "absurdity" in connection with the study of such forms. The present Instruction was meant to put an end to the confusion which his article created. Cf. H. Fesquet, "Nouvelles querelles dans les milieux romains de la critique biblique," *Le Monde* 1 November 1961, p. 8.

Second, it is not so much a question of ensuring at all costs the historical character of every Gospel verse as it is of ascertaining the *way* in which truth has been there presented. One must be more concerned about a better understanding of the peculiar *nature* of the testimony borne to Jesus Christ in the Gospels.

Paragraph IV has thus dealt with the principles, whereas par. V turns to the concrete use of the form-critical method in the study of the Gospels. This method was developed by scholars at the beginning of this century in answer to certain definite problems. Today, it is no longer a purely methodological theory, but has acquired an adult stature. Its infant stages, however, developed only with the most meager involvement of Catholic interpreters; and today the latter bring certain distinctions into the discussion of it. For this reason par. V distinguishes clearly between the "reasonable elements" (*sana elementa*) in the method itself and the questionable "philosophical and theological principles." Such presuppositions have often been closely linked with the method itself and tended to vitiate its conclusions; but they can be separated and have often been so separated in more recent decades. It is impossible to explain the method itself or the questionable presuppositions here in detail.[26] One should merely note that the six specific presuppositions or "principles" listed in the Instruction are normally rejected by Catholic interpreters in any

---

26. For a brief description and discussion of the problems involved, see A. Wikenhauser, *New Testament Introduction* (New York: Herder and Herder, 1958) 253–77; and, better still, A. Wikenhauser and J. Schmid, *Einleitung in das Neue Testament* (6th ed.; Freiburg im B.: Herder, 1973) 290–96. Or J. L. Price, *Interpreting the New Testament* (2nd ed.; New York: Holt, Rinehart and Winston, 1971) 160–82; A. H. McNeile, *An Introduction to the Study of the New Testament* (rev. ed. C. S. C. Williams; Oxford: Clarendon, 1953) 46–58; K. Koch, *The Growth of the Biblical Tradition: The Form-Critical Method* (New York: Scribner, 1969) [for application to Old Testament interpretation]; X. Léon-Dufour, "La lecture critique des évangiles," *Introduction à la Bible: Édition nouvelle* (ed. A. George and P. Grelot; Paris: Desclée) 3/2 (1976) 187–207; A. Robert and A. Feuillet, *Introduction to the New Testament* (New York: Desclée, 1965) 287–310; Bp. J.-J. Weber, " 'Formgeschichte': Wert und Grenzen dieser Methode für das Neue Testament," *TheolGeg* 6 (1963) 63–72; reprinted, *Herderkorrespondenz* 17 (1962–63) 425–29.

case, since many of them are the heritage of rationalism: (1) the denial of a supernatural order; (2) the denial of God's intervention in the
world in strict revelation; (3) the denial of the possibility and existence of miracles; (4) the incompatibility of faith with historical
truth; (5) an almost a priori denial of the historical value and nature
of the documents of revelation; (6) a disdain for apostolic testimony
and undue emphasis on the creative community in the early
Church.[27]

Having made this distinction between the "reasonable elements" and the "philosophical and theological principles" of past
form-critical study, the Biblical Commission goes on in par. VI to
another, more important distinction, which is really the fruit of a
sane use of this method as applied to the Gospels. This is *the* distinction for which this Instruction has rightly been praised. It concerns
the "three stages" of the Gospel tradition: (I) the origin of the traditional material in the dealings of Jesus with his disciples during his
ministry; (II) the passing on and the forming of the material in early
apostolic preaching; and (III) the shaping of it into written Gospels

---

27. The sixth item seems to be directed against the original German Protestant
form critics, whose ideas of *Gemeindetheologie* (community-theology) are apparently
being repudiated. See V. T. O'Keefe, "Towards Understanding the Gospels," *CBQ* 21
(1959) 171–89.

There is, of course, a sense in which it is legitimate to say that the early Christian
community "created" a story about Jesus. Take, for instance, the question of divorce.
The *Sitz im Leben* in the early church(es) may well have been a debate or the solving
of some specific case of conscience ("Do we Christians permit divorce or not?").
Words of Jesus on the subject were recalled, and the story (as in Mark 10:2–12 [minus
the Marcan adaptation]) was "created" at that time. Such a story was likely to be repeated for a generation with varying modifications—until it became a norm for de-
ciding similar cases and was incorporated into the Gospel tradition proper. For an
attempt to sort out the phases of the tradition about this particular example, see my
article, "The Matthean Divorce Texts and Some New Palestinian Evidence," *TS* 37
(1976) 197–226; reprinted, *To Advance the Gospel: New Testament Studies* (New York:
Crossroad, 1981) 79–111.

A difficulty is that the expression "created" often connotes fabrication out of
whole cloth. For this reason it is perhaps wiser to speak of the "formation" of the
story in the early Church rather than of its "creation."

by evangelists. This view of the Gospel tradition is adopted by the
Commission from previous use of it by Roman Catholic scholars.[28] It
enables one to evaluate "the nature of Gospel testimony, the religious life of the early churches, and the sense and value of apostolic
tradition" (par. IV).

The Instruction speaks of "three stages of tradition" (*tria tem-
pora traditionis*). What is meant has often been referred to by other
terms, a difference which serves to bring out other aspects of the
problem and its history. Some writers have spoken of three levels of
comprehension according to which the Gospel text is to be understood; others speak of the three *contexts* of the Gospel material. In
the latter case, the expression is a development of the original idea of
the *Sitz im Leben* of the German form-critical pioneers. After the
First World War they tried to assign to the various Gospel stories
and episodes a *Sitz im Leben,* a "vital context" in the early Church
which would have given rise to the story, unit, or episode. For these
pioneers, *Sitz im Leben* meant *Sitz im Leben der Kirche,* the setting in
the life of the early Church. In time, as the debate developed, people
began to ask about the *Sitz im Leben Jesu,* the vital context in the
ministry of Jesus, in which the saying or episode might have had its
origin in some form or other. Obviously, to recapture this setting
with any certainty is a very delicate and difficult undertaking. Finally, modeled on these two *Sitze im Leben* was a third, which is only
analogous. Granted that questions about the vital context in the ear-

---

28. It would be impossible—and really idle—to try to cite all the Catholic exe-
getes who have used this distinction in modern times. As an example of some who
antedated the Biblical Commission, see J. Dupont, *Les béatitudes* (2nd ed.; Bruges:
Abbaye de Saint-André, 1958); B. M. Ahern, "The Gospels in the Light of Modern
Research," *ChicStud* 1 (1962) 5–16; D. M. Stanley, "Balaam's Ass, or a Problem in
New Testament Hermeneutics," *CBQ* 20 (1958) 50–56; J. A. Fitzmyer, "The Spiritual
Exercises of St. Ignatius and Recent Gospel Study," *Woodstock Letters* 91 (1962) 246–
74; reprinted *Jesuit Spirit in a Time of Change* (ed. R. A. Schroth et al.; Westminster,
Md.: Newman, 1968) 153–81.

For a more recent use of the distinction, see R. E. Brown et al. (eds.), *Peter in the
New Testament* (New York: Paulist; Minneapolis: Augsburg, 1973) 10–11.

ly Church or in Jesus' ministry might be legitimate and instructive, nevertheless the important thing is the *Sitz im Evangelium,* the Gospel context of the saying or event recorded: How did the evangelist make use of the traditional material which he had inherited or received? No matter what name one might prefer for the three stages or their respective nuances, the same issue is involved: In order to understand what the inspired, canonical Gospels are telling us about the life and teaching of Jesus of Nazareth, who has become for Christians Christ the Lord, one has to make this important threefold distinction. Paragraph VI states this expressly in a topic sentence.

Stage I—Jesus' Life and Teaching

Paragraph VII begins with the italicized words *Christus Dominus . . . ,* using titles which are more properly characteristic of the second stage. It would have been better to speak here of *Iesus Nazarenus.* In any case, this paragraph deals with the things that Jesus of Nazareth actually did and said, with the things that the chosen disciples saw and heard. Here two things are emphasized: (1) What the disciples saw and heard enabled them to give testimony about Jesus' life and teaching. (2) The technique which Jesus used in teaching was accommodation intended to make his words understood and retainable. The first few statements in the paragraph are documented with references to the New Testament. The rest of it is a speculative reconstruction, slightly idyllic, but undoubtedly expressing what is essentially to be recalled about this first stage of the Gospel tradition.

It is the stage of the *ipsissima verba Iesu,* "the very words of Jesus." For Christians it has always somehow seemed to be the stage of the greatest importance. What Jesus himself really said would seem to be more important than what the early Church passed on as his teaching or what the evangelists report as his sayings.[29] And yet, it is

---

29. See further my article, "Belief in Jesus Today," *Commonweal* 101 (1974) 137–42.

noteworthy that the Biblical Commission has not insisted in any way
that what we have in the Gospels is an exact record of this first stage
of the tradition.[30]

Stage II—The Apostles' Preaching

The second stage of the tradition is treated in par. VIII. Once
again the emphasis is put on the testimony of the apostles and the
accommodations which they made in their message to the needs of
those to whom they preached. Even when the Commission says that
the apostles after the resurrection "faithfully explained his life and
words," it appeals significantly enough to none of the Gospels as examples of this faithful explanation, but to a part of one of the speeches of Peter in Acts (10:36–41). Peter's speech (before the conversion
of Cornelius and his household) gives a summary of the ministry of
Jesus. It has been regarded by C. H. Dodd[31] and others as an example of the early Church's kerygmatic preaching. (Mark, the earliest
of the canonical Gospels, has even been thought to be an expansion
of some such summary outline.) Strikingly enough, though no
"words" of Jesus are quoted in this speech of Peter,[32] it is still regarded by the Biblical Commission as a "faithful" explanation of Jesus'
"life and words." This nuance is not to be overlooked.

In this section the Commission rightly counteracts the idea that
the new faith of the apostles after the resurrection and the experience

---

30. See p. 22 above.

31. *The Apostolic Preaching and Its Developments* (London: Hodder and Stough-
ton, 1936; reprinted New York: Harper, 1962). For another view of this matter, see U.
Wilckens, *Die Missionsreden der Apostelgeschichte* (WMANT 5; Neukirchen-Vluyn:
Neukirchener-V., 1961) 63–70; but cf. J. Dupont, "Les discours missionnaires des
Actes des Apôtres: D'après un ouvrage récent," *RB* 69 (1962) 37–60, esp. pp. 39–50.

32. Note, by way of contrast, Acts 20:35, where a saying of Jesus is recorded,
which did not find its way into the canonical Gospel tradition.

of Pentecost wiped out all authentic recollection of what Jesus did and said, or deformed their impression of him, or volatilized him into some kind of a "mythical" person. The Commission seeks to stress that the New Testament writings, for all their proclamation of Jesus as Lord, assert the fundamental continuity between Jesus of Nazareth and Jesus Christ as Lord. Jesus, the preacher, may well have become the preached One, but this has not developed merely by a Hellenistic process of mythical apotheosis.

Though this questionable conception of the risen Jesus is rejected, the Commission insists that the apostles passed on what Jesus had actually said and done "with that fuller understanding which they enjoyed" as a result of the experience they went through at the first Easter and of the illumination of the Spirit of Truth at Pentecost. Obvious examples of this fuller understanding are quoted from the Johannine Gospel (2:22; 12:16; 11:51–52). While these instances are explicitly so identified in the Johannine text itself, the Commission does not imply that this fuller understanding is limited only to these three passages. Rather, it emphasizes that the apostles made accommodations to the needs of the audiences which led them to rephrase Jesus' sayings and recast their stories about him. Certainly, *some* differences in the Synoptic tradition are owing to this sort of accommodation, which affected the oral tradition in the pre-literary stage—no matter how much leeway one may want to accord the evangelists themselves in the third stage.

Paragraph VIII ends with the mention of "various modes of speaking" which the apostles used in their ministry and preaching. Because they had to speak to "Greeks and barbarians, the wise and the foolish," such contact influenced them and naturally caused further adaptations of the message which they were preaching. By insisting that the "literary forms" employed in such adaptation must be distinguished and properly assessed (*distinguendi et perpendendi sunt*), the Commission has clearly in mind the use of the form-critical method. The forms which are specifically mentioned in the Instruction ("catecheses, stories,[33] testimonia, hymns, doxologies, prayers") are indeed found in the New Testament, but they are not all used in the Gospels, at least in any abundance. (One thinks more readily of genealogies, parables, miracle-stories, wisdom-sayings, appearance-stories, infancy narratives, etc.) However, the point is made that various literary forms did develop in this stage of the Christian tradition, and that the student of the Gospels must learn to distinguish them and assess them. Still more important is the admission by the Commission that there are other forms not specifically mentioned (*aliaeque id genus formae litterariae*), such as were used by the people of that time.

Stage III — The Evangelists' Writing

The longest exposition in the Instruction is devoted to the third stage of the Gospel tradition in par. IX. What strikes one here is the emphasis laid on the evangelists' "method suited to the peculiar purpose which each one set for himself." The Commission speaks explicitly of *auctores sacri*, "sacred writers," and leaves the question open whether any of the evangelists might themselves have been "apostles," those of whom it speaks in Stage II. (I speak of "evangelists" without prejudice to that distinction.) The Biblical Commission reckons with a process of selection, synthesis, and explication at this stage of the Gospel tradition. From the stories and sayings which cir-

---

33. The Latin word used in the Instruction is *narrationes,* which some may prefer to translate as "narratives." In par. IX it occurs in the singular in the sense of "account," because of its allusion to Luke 1:1. But neither "narrative" nor "account" sufficiently conveys the idea of a literary form, whereas "story" does. It may be objected that this word is "loaded," connoting "fable, fairy tale," etc. True, it often has this connotation, but not always, nor even necessarily. In the long run, the word "story" does not necessarily connote fiction any more than "narrative" connotes what is factual. I am using "story" without implying any pejorative connotation or value judgment.

culated in stage II the evangelists selected material to suit their purposes, synthesized it by topical arrangement, and explicated *(explanantes)* it to suit the needs of the Christian communities for which they compiled their Gospels. Adaptation to the needs of the readers also influenced the process at this stage. Because the evangelists often transposed episodes to a new context, the interpreter must seek out the meaning intended by the evangelist in narrating a story or recounting a saying of Jesus in the chosen context. In saying this, the Commission has implicitly reckoned again not only with form criticism, but also with redaction criticism, a phase of modern Gospel-study which has built upon and added to the earlier form-critical method. Whereas the latter was interested in the history of the literary form (i.e., what the form is and how its development can be discerned as it moves through the tradition), redaction criticism seeks to trace the redactional or editorial history of a saying or episode: How has a given evangelist editorially modified what he has inherited from the tradition before him, and to what purpose (literary, historical, or theological)? This kind of critical study often reveals much about the theological purpose of the evangelist and tells us about the kind of literary portrait of Jesus which he has been seeking to paint, as he utilized and modified inherited material.

After the exhortation to the exegete to ferret out *the evangelist's* meaning, the Commission makes a statement about the "truth" involved in such a process of redaction: "For the truth of the story (*or* narrative, if one insists) is not at all affected by the fact that the evangelists relate the words and deeds of Jesus in a different order and express his sayings not literally but differently, while preserving their sense." The Commission speaks here of "truth" only and does not specify it as "historical truth." One would have to ask what the adjective "historical" would mean in this context after the affirmation of the redactional modifications practiced by the evangelists. One could, of course, then ask, "Well, if it is not a question of historical truth, of what kind is it?" And the answer would have to be, "Gospel-truth."[34] (The discussion in par. X will bear this out.) Paragraph IX ends with a quotation from St. Augustine, which, even though it comes from a writer who holds a less sophisticated view of the Gospels than that being advocated in this Instruction, is nuanced enough to be pertinent to the question. Augustine clearly affirms no naive understanding of the "historical truth" of the Gospels. His words as quoted could never support a simplistic equation of stage III of the Gospel tradition with stage I thereof.

In par. X, which ends the discussion of the three distinct stages of the Gospel tradition, the Commission insists that the interpreter will not be fulfilling his task unless he pays careful attention to all the facets of that tradition. It clearly implies, moreover, that the distinction itself is the result of the "laudable achievements of recent research." Then follows this significant statement: "From the results of

---

34. This answer may, of course, sound facetious. It is *not* meant in the sense in which we commonly use this expression in English: "Now I'll tell you the gospel-truth about that." (When this commentary of mine was translated into German as Stuttgarter Bibelstudien 1, I warned one of the editors of the series that this answer would be misunderstood in German, unless he sought some way of explaining it. That proved impossible. The booklet was eventually reviewed by O. Loretz in *TRev* 63 (1967) 1–8, an Old Testament professor who perhaps should be pardoned for what he wrote, but his smugness in criticizing my comments revealed that he had completely missed the point.)

I intend the phrase the "Gospel truth" to be taken in a serious way, which the very form of Gospel demands. After all truth is analogous; or, as A. Cardinal Bea once put it, "Sua cuique generi literario est veritas," "Each literary form has its own truth" (*De Scripturae sacrae inspiratione* [2nd ed.: Rome: Biblical Institute, 1935] 106 §90). Truth in a literary text is gauged by the form of genre employed; one has to distinguish historical truth from poetic, rhetorical truth from epistolary, hortatory truth from prayer-truth (as in the psalter), and legal truth from mythical. In this sense it is legitimate to speak of "gospel-truth," i.e., that religious and salutary truth expressed by the evangelist which may indeed make use of historical, or genealogical, or hortatory truth, or what have you. Since it is difficult to define what a gospel is, it is equally difficult to specify properly in what the gospel-truth may consist. In any case, it is not simply identical with "historical truth" in some fundamentalistic sense.

the new investigations it is apparent that the doctrine and the life of Jesus were not simply reported for the sole purpose of being remembered, but were 'preached' so as to offer the Church a basis of faith and of morals. . . ."[35] The Commission implies thereby that the "Gospel-truth" is not tied to any fundamentalistic literalness or superior quality of apostolic recollections or reminiscences.

The last paragraph addressed to the exegetes (XI) begins with an admission that there are still many serious problems on which the exegete "can and must freely (*libere*) exercise his skill and genius." The admission about the freedom of exegetical research is a repetition of the statement of Pius XII about the liberty of the Catholic exegete in *Divino afflante Spiritu*. The statement in the Instruction, however, is a paraphrase and contains a significant addition which spells out the relationship of the work of exegetes in the Catholic Church to the magisterium or teaching authority in the Church. We juxtapose the two texts:

Divino afflante Spiritu	*Instructio*
There remain therefore many things, and of the greatest importance, in the discussion and exposition of which the skill and genius of Catholic commentators may and ought to be freely exercised, so that each may contribute his part to the advantage of all, to the continued progress of sacred doctrine,	There are still many things, and of the greatest importance, in the discussion and exposition of which the Catholic exegete can and must freely exercise his skill and genius so that each may contribute his part to the advantage of all, to the continued progress of sacred doctrine, to the preparation and further sup-

---

35. The Latin text of this sentence reads: "Cum ex eis quae novae inquisitiones contulerunt appareat doctrinam et vitam Iesu non simpliciter relatas fuisse, eo solo fine ut memoria tenerentur, sed 'praedicatas' fuisse ita ut Ecclesiae fundamentum fidei et morum praeberent, interpres testimonium Evangelistarum indefesse perscrutans, vim theologicam perennem Evangeliorum altius illustrare et quantae sit Ecclesiae interpretatio necessitatis quantique momenti in plena luce collocare valebit" (par. X).

port of the judgment to be exercised by the ecclesiastical
and to the defense and honor of the   magisterium, and to the defense
Church.[36]   and honor of the Church. (Par. XI)

What emerges here in the text of the Instruction is some of the new insights and experiences of Vatican Council II, similar to the awareness expressed by Pope John Paul II in his address at The Catholic University of America in 1979.[37]

The exegetes are finally urged to be ready to submit to the directives of the magisterium, never to forget that the apostles filled with the Holy Spirit preached the good news, and that the evangelists were inspired so that they were preserved "from all error." This final exhortation is supported by a quotation from Irenaeus. So end the directives to the exegetes.

---

36. *AAS* 35 (1943) 319; *EnchBib* §565; the translation is from *RSS*, 102. The juxtaposed Latin texts read:

Divino afflante Spiritu	*Instructio*
Multa igitur remanent, eaque gravissima in quibus edisserendis et explanandis catholicorum interpretum acumen et ingenium libere exerceri potest et debet, ut ad omnium utilitatem, ad maiorem in dies doctrinae sacrae profectum et ad Ecclesiae defensionem et honorem ex suo quisque viritim conferat.	Multa supersunt eaque gravissima in quibus edisserendis et explanandis exegeta catholicus acumen et ingenium libere exercere potest et debet, ut ad omnium utilitatem, ad maiorem in dies doctrinae sacrae profectum, ad iudicium magisterii Ecclesiae praeparandum et ulterius fulciendum, ad Ecclesiae defensionem et honorem ex suo quisque viritim conferat. (The text of the Instruction refers to DaS n. 27.)

37. See my discussion in "John Paul II, Academic Freedom and the Magisterium," *America* 141 (1979) 247–49.

To Professors of Scripture in Seminaries and Similar Institutions

The directives addressed to Scripture professors in seminaries and similar institutions (par. XII) consist of an exhortation to teach Scripture in a way that the dignity of the subject and the needs of the time require. Coming immediately after the directives to the exegetes, who have been encouraged to pursue a form-critical and redaction-critical interpretation of the Gospels, this exhortation implies the seminary professors' duty to cope with the same methods and to engage in the same research. Indeed, this is part of the "needs of the time" (*temporum necessitas*), and such professors cannot ignore them. In reality, the distinction made between exegetes and seminary professors in this Instruction is largely abstract; the exegete is invariably a professor in a seminary or a similar institution. On the other hand, when the seminary professor is not engaged in such research, such a situation cries out for reform.

The Commission, however, insists that the use of such methods of literary criticism is not an end in itself. They must be used to bring out the meaning of the Gospel passages intended by God through the sacred writers. The professor is above all to emphasize the theological or religious teaching of the Gospels, and literary criticism is to serve only as a means to set forth the theological teaching of the evangelists.[38] Those whom seminary professors are training are fu-

---

38. In the light of these directives it is difficult to understand how some interpreters today can recommend that one abandon the historical-critical method of interpreting the Gospels. All through the Instruction it is clear that the modern Catholic exegete and seminary professor are counseled to ascertain and explain what the intention of the inspired writer was and what meaning his message has for people in the world of today. The Instruction has not envisaged more recent fads and trends in interpretation, such as structuralism, or those in hermeneutics, such as the recommendation that what is important is not the intended meaning of the author but what the text, having acquired an autonomy of its own—so it is alleged—may mean to readers today. If there is not a radical homogeneity between what it meant and what it means today, then the latter cannot be called "the Christian message." How a concern for the latter and a disregard of the former can be called serious literary criticism is baffling.

ture priests and future ministers of the Church, for whose lives and work the Scriptures must be *the* source of perennial vitality.

The exhortation in par. XII is predominantly positive. The only negative element in it is a warning against the pursuit of the literary criticism of the Gospels as if this could be conceived of as an end in itself.

To Preachers

In the case of preachers the Biblical Commission first insists on their preaching of "doctrine," appealing to 1 Tim 4:16 (par. XIII). The first strong, negative directives of the entire Instruction appear here: "They are to refrain entirely from proposing idle and insufficiently established novelties." This prohibition, however, has to be properly understood; for immediately afterward the Commission itself allows for the cautious explanation of "new opinions already solidly established." The problem is obvious. There cannot be a double standard of truth, one for exegetes and seminary Scripture professors, and another for the faithful. If I am correct in my understanding of this Instruction, then the recognition which the Biblical Commission has given to literary forms and to the sane use of form-critical and redaction-critical interpretation of the Gospels would put the results of such study under the "opinions already solidly established." They are indeed to be explained to the faithful. But whether one does this in the pulpit, as a preacher at the liturgy of the word, or in an instruction-class, is a matter of prudential judgment.

The directives to preachers end with another caution: They are not to embellish biblical events with imaginative details scarcely consonant with the truth.

To Those Who Publish for the Faithful

The same prudence demanded of preachers is now required of all those who would write on biblical subjects at a popular level (par.

XIV). They are to concentrate on the riches of God's word and are to consider it a sacred duty never to depart from the common teaching and tradition of the Church. They are to exploit, however, the findings of modern biblical research, yet avoiding "the rash comments of innovators." A "pernicious itch for novelty" is not to lead them to disseminate unwisely what are only trial solutions to classic difficulties.

The Commission further recalls (par. XV) that books and articles in magazines and newspapers on biblical subjects are to be carefully scrutinized by ordinaries (i.e., diocesan bishops and similar superiors).

To Biblical Associations

Directors of biblical associations or societies are to follow the norms for such gatherings laid down by the Biblical Commission on a previous occasion (para. XVI).[39]

Conclusion of the Instruction

The Biblical Commission notes in conclusion (par. XVII) that if all the directives set forth in its Instruction were to be followed, then the study of Sacred Scripture in the Church would greatly contribute to the benefit of all the faithful. It ends with a quotation from 2 Tim 3:15–17, the classic New Testament passage setting forth the purpose of "all Scripture divinely inspired."

Final Remarks

The significance of this Instruction of the Biblical Commission in 1964 is best understood in the light of events which had been taking place in the Roman Catholic Church either shortly before its

---

39. *EnchBib* §622–33; *RSS,* 168–72.

publication or contemporary with it, for it was issued during the course of Vatican Council II and all that that meant for the Church. As one looks back at that time from the early 1980's one can see even greater significance.

Shortly before the publication of the Instruction there emerged a rather bitter strife between some professors at the Lateran University in Rome and those of the Biblical Institute, which centered on aspects of the problem with which the Instruction was eventually to deal—"new investigations" (*novae investigationes,* par. X) of the Gospels and other biblical books. That strife need not be rehearsed here;[40] but it was unfortunate because it obscured the important issue of the historical truth of the Bible.

In addition, there were mixed reactions, reported from all over the world, to the new trends in modern Catholic biblical studies. Conservative ecclesiastical circles, in Rome and elsewhere, sought— and still do seek—to commit Catholic interpretation of the Gospels to fundamentalism.[41] In this context, the well-nuanced position which the Biblical Commission took in this Instruction is of greatest

---

40. See my article, "A Recent Roman Scriptural Controversy," *TS* 22 (1961) 426–44.

41. The first draft of the schema *De fontibus revelationis,* prepared by the theological commission for discussion at Vatican Council II, contained two paragraphs which incorporated the terminology of the *monitum* of the Holy Office (1961) and leveled anathemas against those who would call in question the proper historical and objective truth of the words and deeds of Jesus *prouti narrantur* ("as they are recounted"). These paragraphs were eventually rejected along with the rest of that schema. See J. Ratzinger, "Dogmatic Constitution on Divine Revelation: Origin and Background," *Commentary on the Documents of Vatican II* (5 vols.; ed. H. Vorgrimler; New York: Herder and Herder, 1967–69) 3 (1968) 155–66; cf. A. Grillmeier, "The Divine Inspiration and the Interpretation of Sacred Scripture," ibid., 199–246; B. Rigaux, "The New Testament," ibid., 252–61 (esp. pp. 258–59 on the eventual rejection of a papal suggestion to use *vera seu historica fide digna* instead of *vera et sincera* [which was eventually retained]). In contrast to the original schema, what appears in *Dei verbum* §19 is rather a brief summary of the Biblical Commission's Instruction (see p. 141 below).

importance. It not only did not espouse any form of fundamentalism, but gave, in effect, official sanction to many of the new trends in biblical study, and especially in Gospel study.[42]

On the other hand, the silence of the Commission about certain matters raises several questions. *First,* practically nothing is said in the Instruction about the Synoptic problem, i.e., about how the Synoptic Gospels are related to or dependent on each other (see p. 9 above). True, in dealing with the redactional work of the evangelists, the Commission admitted that they had used a "method suited to the peculiar purpose which each set for himself," and selected, synthesized, explicated, or transposed accordingly. Obviously, the Commission did not want to take sides in the debate about the solution to the problem which is so contested today.[43] This knotty problem will

---

42. Though the main directives in the Instruction have been addressed to exegetes, it is evident that dogmatic theologians and others have also had to reckon with the directives of this document. We smile today in retrospect at the confidence behind the remarks directed against a professor at the Biblical Institute in Rome in the year 1962, which stated that "there exists a numerous and fairly articulate group convinced that the four Gospels and the Acts of the Apostles are genuine and objectively accurate historical documents, which can be used as such legitimately in the science of apologetics. These individuals insist that they have reason to hold and to teach that the events set forth in these books took place in the very way in which they are described in these works. They hold that the words and the deeds attributed to Our Lord were actually uttered and performed by Him . . ." (J. C. Fenton, "Father Moran's Prediction," *AER* 146 [1962] 192–201, esp. pp 194–95). Not only is such a view of things contrary to the Instruction of the Biblical Commission, but it displays a naïveté which seems never to have heard of the Synoptic problem, not to mention form and redaction criticism.

On the other hand, it is evident that more recent dogmatic theologians, in their discussions of christology, have actually been seeking to cope with the thrust of the Instruction. See W. Kasper, *Jesus the Christ* (London: Burns & Oates, 1976) 26–40; E. Schillebeeckx, *Jesus* (New York: Seabury, 1979); *Christ* (New York: Crossroad, 1981).

43. See further my article, "The Priority of Mark and the 'Q' Source in Luke," *Jesus and Man's Hope* (Perspective Books, 1; 2 vols.; Pittsburgh: Pittsburgh Theological Seminary, 1970) 1. 131–70; reprinted (in revised form), *To Advance the Gospel* (see n. 27 above), 3–40.

probably never be solved to the complete satisfaction of everyone, and the Instruction leaves the debate on this issue open. But the silence of the Commission on this question has made some of its statements sound like an oversimplification, as non-Catholic readers of the Instruction may notice. How can one discuss the problem of the historical value of the Gospels without assuming—or at least recognizing—some position in this matter? In speculating about the reasons for the silence of the Commission in this area, I have already suggested that the Commission apparently thought that it could give directives in a way sufficiently generic so as not to close debate on solutions to the Synoptic problem.

Second, there is the question of the reinterpretation of the words of Jesus by the evangelists in their redactional work. It has often been suggested in recent times that the evangelists have put on the lips of Jesus a fuller form of sayings than his *ipsissima verba,* or that certain verses are to be regarded as the redactional addition(s) of the evangelists. We may cite the Matthean additions to the beatitudes,[44] and to the "Our Father," or the exceptive phrases in the divorce texts of the Gospel tradition,[45] or even the very knotty problem of Matt 16:16b–19.[46] Significantly, the Commission has not come out against such views in Catholic biblical studies in an otherwise comprehensive statement on the "historical truth of the Gospels." Indeed, the Commission is undoubtedly hinting at *this kind* of

---

44. Compare Luke's "Blessed are you poor" with Matthew's "Blessed are the poor in spirit," Luke's "Blessed are you that hunger now" with Matthew's "Blessed are those who hunger and thirst for uprightness," etc. See the admirable treatment of this question by J. Dupont, *Les béatitudes* (see n. 28 above), 209–27; also M. M. Bourke, "The Historicity of the Gospels," *Thought* 39 (1964) 37–56; J. A. Fitzmyer, *The Gospel According to Luke I–IX* (AB 28; Garden City, N.Y.: Doubleday, 1981) 631.

45. See my article cited in n. 27 above, esp. pp. 87–89.

46. See now R. E. Brown et al. (eds) *Peter in the New Testament* (see n. 28 above), 83–101; cf. A. Vögtle, "Messiasbekenntnis und Petrusverheissung: Zur Komposition Mt 16, 13–23 Par.," *BZ* ns 1 (1957) 252–72; 2 (1958) 85–103; T. de Kruijf, *Der Sohn des lebendigen Gottes* (AnBib 16; Rome: Biblical Institute, 1962) 82; E. F. Sutcliffe, "St. Peter's Double Confession in Mt 16:16–19," *HeyJ* 3 (1962) 31–41.

redactional activity involved in the reinterpretation of the words of Jesus, when it says: "From the many things handed down they selected some things, reduced others to a synthesis, (still) *others they explicated as they kept in mind the situation of the churches*" (par. IX, my italics). Such an unfolding, explanation, or explication of traditional material for the situation of various local churches has to be reckoned with. For instance, the addition of the exceptive phrases in the divorce texts of Matt 5:32 and 19:9 may well reflect a marriage problem in an early Christian community, predominantly Jewish Christian, but being infiltrated by converts from the Gentile world already in marital situations for which the evangelist expresses an exception (cf. Acts 15:20,29; 21:25).[47] The attitude reflected in the Instruction toward this type of problem is most significant.

Third, in a Church document on the historical value of the Gospels one would have thought that something would have been said about the historical character of the infancy narratives of Matthew and Luke. The debate about this part of the Gospel tradition was already a live one within Roman Catholicism before the Instruction was issued and before the debate on inspiration and inerrancy at Vatican Council II. The silence of the Commission on this matter, especially in its treatment of Stage I of the Gospel tradition, is eloquent indeed.[48]

---

47. See P. Benoit, *L'Evangile selon saint Matthieu* (La sainte Bible [de Jérusalem]; 3d ed.; Paris: Cerf, 1961) 121; H. J. Richards, "Christ on Divorce," *Scr* 11 (1959) 22–32; cf. n. 45 above.

48. The same would have to be said about *Dei Verbum* §19; cf. R. E. Brown, *The Birth of the Messiah: A Commentary on the Infancy Narratives in Matthew and Luke* (Garden City, N.Y.: Doubleday, 1977) 562, esp. n. 11.

For another view of this matter, see J. Redford, "The Quest of the Historical Epiphany: Critical Reflections on Raymond Brown's 'The Birth of the Messiah,'" *Clergy Review* 64 (1979) 5–11. The "critical reflections" amount to nothing more than another gratuitous assertion about the historical character of the annunciation, summed up in a question to boot: ". . . what is more feasible than that he [Luke] had to hand a tradition, oral or written, of the infancy of Jesus whose original source was Mary, whether she was personally with Luke or not at the time of writing?" (p. 9). Alas, a rhetorical question is no basis of historicity.

Fourth, most noteworthy in the whole document, when all is said and done, is that *the Biblical Commission calmly and frankly admitted that what is contained in the Gospels as we have them today is not the record of the words and deeds of Jesus in the first stage of the tradition, nor even the form in which they were preached in the second stage, but only the form compiled and edited by the evangelists.* This form, however, reflects with a certain fidelity the two previous stages, to be sure, and the second more than the first.

For the believing Christian and scholar, it is important to note that the evangelists' redacted and edited form of the sayings and deeds of Jesus is precisely the inspired form. The evangelists were moved by the Holy Spirit to compile, edit, and write down the accounts as they did. This inspiration guarantees their Gospel-truth, which is free from error.

It is good, however, to recall that neither the Church in its official pronouncements about the nature of inspiration nor theologians in their speculative elaborations have ever taught that the necessary formal effect of inspiration is historicity. The consequence of inspiration is inerrancy in affirmation, i.e., immunity from error in what is affirmed or taught in the sacred writings for the sake of our salvation (see *Dei Verbum* §11). The opposite of such error is not simply historicity, but truth. Yet truth in a literary text is analogous to the literary form used (see n. 34 above). If a passage in the Gospels contains historical truth, it does not simply contain it because it is inspired. The reasons for its historical character will be quite other than the inspired character of the text. Inspiration may indeed guarantee such historical truth as is there, even as it would guarantee the poetic truth of what is affirmed in the hymn to Christ in Phil 2:6–11. The guarantee is not quantitative, but qualitative and analogous. This has to be stressed even when something is narrated in the past tense under inspiration. The first question which confronts the interpreter in such a case as Mark 14:52 ("and he [the youth] relinquished the linen cloth and ran away naked") is whether that statement is meant to record an historical event (real naked flight) or to convey symbolism (the *utter* dereliction of Jesus by his followers); similarly for Mark 15:38 ("the veil in the temple was torn in two, from top to bottom").

Lastly, the inspired truth of the Gospels was intended by God in his providence to give us not simply a "remembered" account of the life and teaching of Jesus, but a "preached" form of it, "so as to offer the Church a basis of faith and morals" (par. X).

The Instruction of the Biblical Commission has by no means put an end to all the problems regarding the historicity of the Gospels. Discussion of them has continued and will certainly carry on, but now with much more freedom. The Instruction has occasioned a number of commentaries on it; we append a list of the more important ones as an aid to further study of it and of the problems to which it is addressed.[49]

49. Anon., "Instruktion der päpstlichen Bibelkommission," *Kirchenblatt für die reformierte Schweiz* 120 (1964) 233–34; A. Bea, "La storicità dei vangeli sinottici," *CivC* 115/2 (1964) 417–36; "Il carattere storico dei vangeli sinottici come opere ispirate," ibid., 526–45 (both reprinted separately, Rome: Civiltà cattolica, 1964; reprinted again with an Italian translation of the Instruction, *La storicità dei vangeli* [Brescia: Morcelliana, 1964]; cf. *The Study of the Synoptic Gospels: New Approaches and Outlooks* [New York: Harper & Row, 1965]); F. W. Beare, "The Historical Truth of the Gospels: An Official Pronouncement of the Pontifical Biblical Commission," *CJT* 11 (1965) 231–37; W. Beilner, "Zur Instruktion der Bibelkommission über die historische Wahrheit der Evangelien," *BLit* 38 (1964–65) 3–5; "Die Geschichtlichkeit der Evangelien," *BLit* 40 (1967) 159–76; R. Cardinaels, "Bijbelcomissie en Evangelie," *Revue ecclésiastique de Liège* 50 (1964) 271–81; J. Delorme, "La vérité historique des évangiles," *L'Ami du clergé* 74 (1964) 554–59; M. Didier, "Liminaire [à l'Instruction]," *RDiocNam* 18 (1964) 309–12; A. de la Fuente, "Documento alentador para los estudios de la Biblia," *Ecclesia* 24 (1964) 1103–6; E. Galbiati, "L'Istruzione della Commissione Biblica sul valore storico degli Evangeli," *BeO* 6 (1964) 233–45; "L'Istruzione della Commissione Biblica sul valore storico dei Vangeli," *ScCatt* 92 (1964) 303–310; "L'Istruzione sulla verità storica dei Vangeli e l'insegnamento nei seminari," *Seminarium* 18 (1966) 66–91; S. Gonzáles de Carrea, "El método histórico-redaccional en los evangelios sinópticos," *Natura et gratia* 11 (1964) 205–25; W. Harrington, "The Instruction on the Historical Truth of the Gospels," *IER* 103 (1965) 73–87; F. Hoyos, "Historia e historias: A propósito de la instrucción de la Comisión Bíblica," *RevistB* 27 (1965) 67–73; J. Kahmann, " 'De historica evangeliorum veritate,' Een nieuwe Instructie van de Bijbelcommissie," *Nederlandsche katholieke Stemmen* 61 (1965) 46–51; C. Kearns, "The Instruction on the Historical Truth of the

The text of the Instruction itself follows.[50] After it will be found a translation of *Dei verbum* §19, which restated in a brief conciliar form the teaching of the Instruction of the Biblical Commission, and significantly not that of the *monitum* of the Holy Office of 1961.

Gospels: Some First Impressions," *Ang* 41 (1964) 218–34; O. Knoch, "Über die historische Wahrheit der Evangelien. . .," *BKirche* 19 (1964) 146–50; N. Lohfink, "Die Evangelien und die Geschichte: Zur Instruktion der päpstlichen Bibel-komission vom 21. April 1964," *SdZ* 174 (1964) 365–74 (reprinted, *Theologisches Jahrbuch 1966* (Leipzig: Benno, 1966) 240–48; (an abridged Swedish form appeared in *Credo* 46 [Uppsala, 1965] 29–33); J. Losada, "La verdad histórica de los Evangelios: La instrucción de la Comisión Bíblica," *SalTer* 52 (1964) 612–24, 673–83; R. E. Murphy, "The Biblical Instruction," *Commonweal* 80/14 (1964) 418–20; J. A. O'Flynn, "Instruction of the Biblical Commission," *ITQ* 31 (1964) 240–46; M. Peinador, "Sobre la reciente instrucción de la Comisión Bíblica," *Ilustración del clero* 57 (1964) 718–24; J. Radermakers, "Instruction du 21 avril 1964 sur la vérité historique des évangiles: Commentaire," *NRT* 86 (1964) 640–43; R. Rouquette, "De Rome et de la chrétienté: L'Instruction de la Commission biblique," *Etudes* 321 (1964) 105–10; E. Ruckstuhl, "Die Wahrheit der Evangelien: Erläuterungen zur neuen Instructio der Bibelkommission," *Schwiezerische Kirchenzeitung* 132 (1964) 297–99; M. Sabbe, "Een nieuwe Bijbelinstructie," *ColBG* 10 (1964) 413–19; R. Schnackenburg, "Über die historische Wahrheit der Evangelien: Instruktion der päpstlichen Bibelkommission," *TheolGeg* 7 (1964) 197–109; A. Stöger, "Die historische Wahrheit der Evangelien: Kommentar zur Instruktion der päpstlichen Bibelkommission vom 21. April 1964," *TPQ* 113 (1965) 57–79; J. Díaz y Díaz and P. Termes, "Evangelios y comisión bíblica," *Enciclopedia de la Biblia* (6 vols.; Barcelona: Garriga, 1963), 3. 299–305.

50. The numbering of the footnotes of the Latin text is generally preserved; occasionally it has been necessary to reverse two of them because of the English word-order. Words added in parentheses do not appear in the Latin text; they have been supplied for the sake of the English. See notes 16 and 23 above. For some strange reason the references to the encyclical *Divino afflante Spiritu* are given in the Latin text of the Instruction to the Italian translation of the encyclical in *AAS;* I have changed them to the corresponding pages of the official Latin text.

2.

Instruction: Text

I. Holy Mother the Church "the pillar and bulwark of truth,"[1] has always used Sacred Scripture in her task of imparting heavenly salvation to human beings. She has always defended it, too, from every sort of false interpretation. Since there will never be an end to (biblical) problems, the Catholic exegete should never lose heart in explaining the divine word and in solving the difficulties proposed to him. Rather, let him strive earnestly to open up still more the real meaning of the Scriptures. Let him rely firmly not only on his own resources, but above all on the help of God and the light of the Church.

II. It is a source of great joy that there are found today, to meet the needs of our times, faithful children of the Church in great numbers who are experts in biblical matters. They are following the exhortations of the Supreme Pontiffs and are dedicating themselves wholeheartedly and untiringly to this serious and arduous task. "Let all the other children of the Church bear in mind that the efforts of these resolute laborers in the vineyard of the Lord are to be judged not only with equity and justice, but also with the greatest charity,"[2] since even illustrious interpreters, such as Jerome himself, tried at times to explain the more difficult questions with no great success.[3] Care should be had "that the keen strife of debate should never exceed the bounds of mutual charity. Nor should the impression be giv-

---

1. 1 Tim 3:15.
2. *DaS* 46 (*AAS* 35 [1943] 319; *EnchBib* §564; *RRS,* 101).
3. See *Spiritus Paraclitus* 2, 3 (*AAS* 12 [1920] 392; *EnchBib* §451; *RSS,* 50).

en in an argument that truths of revelation and divine traditions are being called in question. For unless agreement among minds be safeguarded and principles be carefully respected, great progress in this discipline will never be expected from the diverse pursuits of so many persons."[4]

III. Today more than ever the work of exegetes is needed, because many writings are being spread abroad in which the truth of the deeds and words which are contained in the Gospels is questioned. For this reason the Pontifical Biblical Commission, in pursuit of the task given to it by the Supreme Pontiffs, has considered it proper to set forth and insist upon the following points.

IV. 1. Let the Catholic exegete, following the guidance of the Church, derive profit from all that earlier interpreters, especially the holy Fathers and Doctors of the Church, have contributed to the understanding of the sacred text. And let him carry on their labors still further. In order to put the abiding truth and authority of the Gospels in their full light, he will accurately adhere to the norms of rational and Catholic hermeneutics. He will diligently employ the new exegetical aids, above all those which the historical method, taken in its widest sense, offers to him—a method which carefully investigates sources and defines their nature and value, and makes use of such helps as textual criticism, literary criticism, and the study of languages. The interpreter will heed the advice of Pius XII of happy memory, who enjoined him "prudently . . . to examine what contribution the manner of expression or the literary genre used by the sacred writer makes to a true and genuine interpretation. And let him be convinced that this part of his task cannot be neglected without serious detriment to Catholic exegesis."[5] By this piece of advice Pius XII of happy memory enunciated a general rule of hermeneutics by

---

4. Apostolic Letter, *Vigilantiae* (*EnchBib* §143; *RSS*, 33).
5. *DaS* (*AAS* 35 [1943] 316; *EnchBib* §560; *RSS*, 98).

which the books of the Old Testament as well as the New must be explained. For in composing them the sacred writers employed the way of thinking and writing which was in vogue among their contemporaries. Finally, the exegete will use all the means available to probe more deeply into the nature of Gospel testimony, into the religious life of the early churches, and into the sense and the value of apostolic tradition.

V. As occasion warrants, the interpreter may examine what reasonable elements are contained in the "form-critical method" that can be used for a fuller understanding of the Gospels. But let him be wary, because quite inadmissible philosophical and theological principles have often come to be mixed with this method, which not uncommonly have vitiated the method itself as well as the conclusions in the literary area. For some proponents of this method have been led astray by the prejudiced views of rationalism. They refuse to admit the existence of a supernatural order and the intervention of a personal God in the world through strict revelation, and the possibility and existence of miracles and prophecies. Others begin with a false idea of faith, as if it had nothing to do with historical truth—or rather were incompatible with it. Others deny the historical value and nature of the documents of revelation almost a priori. Finally, others make light of the authority of the apostles as witnesses to Christ, and of their task and influence in the primitive community, extolling rather the creative power of that community. All such views are not only opposed to Catholic doctrine, but are also devoid of scientific basis and alien to the correct principles of historical method.

VI. 2. To judge properly concerning the reliability of what is transmitted in the Gospels, the interpreter should pay diligent attention to the three stages of tradition by which the doctrine and the life of Jesus have come down to us.

VII. *Christ our Lord* joined to himself chosen disciples,[6] who followed him from the beginning,[7] saw his deeds, heard his words, and in this way were equipped to be witnesses of his life and doctrine.[8] When the Lord was orally explaining his doctrine, he followed the modes of reasoning and of exposition which were in vogue at the time. He accommodated himself to the mentality of his listeners and saw to it that what he taught was firmly impressed on the mind and easily remembered by the disciples. These people understood the miracles and other events of the life of Jesus correctly, as deeds performed or designed that human beings might believe in Christ through them, and embrace with faith the doctrine of salvation.

VIII. *The apostles* proclaimed above all the death and resurrection of the Lord, as they bore witness to Jesus.[9] They faithfully explained his life and words,[10] while taking into account in their method of preaching the circumstances in which their listeners found themselves.[11] After Jesus rose from the dead and his divinity was clearly perceived,[12] faith, far from destroying the memory of what had transpired, rather confirmed it, because their faith rested on the things which Jesus did and taught.[13] Nor was he changed into a "mythical" person and his teaching deformed in consequence of the worship which the disciples from that time on paid Jesus as the Lord and the Son of God. On the other hand, there is no reason to deny that the apostles passed on to their listeners what was really said and done by the Lord with that fuller understanding which they en-

---

6. Mark 3:14; Luke 6:13.
7. Luke 1:2; Acts 1:21–22.
8. Luke 24:28; John 15:27; Acts 1:8; 10:39; 13:31.
9. Luke 24:44–48; Acts 2:32; 3:15; 5:30–32.
10. Acts 10:36–41.
11. Compare Acts 13:16–41 with Acts 17:22–31.
12. Acts 2:36; John 20:28.
13. Acts 2:22; 10:37–39.

joyed,[14] having been instructed by the glorious events of the Christ and taught by the light of the Spirit of Truth.[15] So, just as Jesus himself after his resurrection "interpreted to them"[16] the words of the Old Testament as well as his own,[17] they too interpreted his words and deeds according to the needs of their listeners. "Devoting themselves to the ministry of the word,"[18] they preached and made use of various modes of speaking which were suited to their own purpose and the mentality of their listeners. For they were debtors[19] "to Greeks and barbarians, to the wise and the foolish."[20] But these modes of speaking with which the preachers proclaimed Christ must be distinguished and (properly) assessed: catecheses, stories, testimonia, hymns, doxologies, prayers—and other literary forms of this sort which were in Sacred Scripture and were accustomed to be used by people of that time.

IX. This primitive instruction, which was at first passed on by word of mouth and then in writing—for it soon happened that many tried "to compile a narrative of the things"[21] which concerned the Lord Jesus—was committed to writing by the sacred authors in four Gospels for the benefit of the churches, with a method suited to the peculiar purpose which each (author) set for himself. From the many things handed down they selected some things, reduced others to a synthesis, (still) others they explicated as they kept in mind the situation of the churches. With every (possible) means they sought that their readers might become aware of the reliability[22] of those words

---

14. John 2:22; 12:16; 11:51–52; cf. 14:26; 16:12–13; 7:39.
15. John 14:26; 16:13.
16. Luke 24:27.
17. Luke 24:44–45; Acts 1:3.
19. 1 Cor 9:19–23.
20. Rom 1:14.
20. Rom 1:14.
21. Luke 1:1.
22. Luke 1:4.

by which they had been instructed. Indeed, from what they had received the sacred writers above all selected the things which were suited to the various situations of the faithful and to the purpose which they had in mind, and adapted their narration of them to the same situations and purpose. Since the meaning of a statement also depends on the sequence, the evangelists, in passing on the words and deeds of our Savior, explained these now in one context, now in another, depending on (their) usefulness to the readers. Consequently, let the exegete seek out the meaning intended by the evangelist in narrating a saying or a deed in a certain way or in placing it in a certain context. For the truth of the story is not at all affected by the fact that the evangelists relate the words and deeds of the Lord in a different order,[23] and express his sayings not literally but differently, while preserving (their) sense.[24] For, as St. Augustine says, "It is quite probable that each evangelist believed it to have been his duty to recount what he had to in that order in which it pleased God to suggest it to his memory—in those things at least in which the order, whether it be this or that, detracts in nothing from the truth and authority of the Gospel. But why the Holy Spirit, who apportions individually to each one as he wills,[25] and who therefore undoubtedly also governed and ruled the minds of the holy (writers) in recalling what they were to write because of the preeminent authority which the books were to enjoy, permitted one to compile his narrative in this way, and another in that, anyone with pious diligence may seek the reason and with divine aid will be able to find it."[26]

X. Unless the exegete pays attention to all these things which pertain to the origin and composition of the Gospels and makes

---

23. See John Chrysostom, *Hom. in Matth.* 1, 3 (*PG* 57. 16–17).

24. Augustine, *De consensu evangelistarum* 2.12,28 (*PL* 34. 1090–91; *CSEL* 43. 127–29).

25. 1 Cor 12:11.

26. *De consensu evangelistarum* 2.21, 51–52 (*PL* 34. 1102; *CSEL* 43. 153).

proper use of all the laudable achievements of recent research, he will not fulfill his task of probing into what the sacred writers intended and what they really said. From the results of the new investigations it is apparent that the doctrine and the life of Jesus were not simply reported for the sole purpose of being remembered, but were "preached" so as to offer the Church a basis of faith and of morals. The interpreter (then), by tirelessly scrutinizing the testimony of the evangelists, will be able to illustrate more profoundly the perennial theological value of the Gospels and bring out clearly how necessary and important the Church's interpretation is.

XI. There are still many things, and of the greatest importance, in the discussion and explanation of which the Catholic exegete can and must freely exercise his skill and genius so that each may contribute his part to the advantage of all, to the continued progress of sacred doctrine, to the preparation and further support of the judgment to be exercised by the ecclesiastical magisterium, and to the defense and honor of the Church.[27] But let him always be disposed to obey the magisterium of the Church and not forget that the apostles, filled with the Holy Spirit, preached the good news, and that the Gospels were written under the inspiration of the Holy Spirit, who preserved their authors from all error. "Now we have not learned of the plan of our salvation from any others than those through whom the Gospel has come to us. Indeed, what they once preached they later passed on to us in the Scriptures by the will of God, as the ground and pillar of our faith. It is not right to say that they preached before they had acquired perfect knowledge, as some would venture to say who boast of being correctors of the apostles. In fact, after our Lord rose from the dead and they were invested with power from on high, as the Holy Spirit came down upon them, they were filled with all (his gifts) and had perfect knowledge. They went forth

---

27. *DaS* 47 (*AAS* 35 [1943] 319; *EnchBib* §565; *RSS,* 102).

to the ends of the earth, one and all with God's Gospel, announcing the news of God's bounty to us and proclaiming heavenly peace to men."[28]

XII. 3. Those whose *task it is to teach in seminaries and similar institutions* should have it as their "prime concern that ... Holy Scripture be so taught as both the dignity of the discipline and the needs of the times require."[29] Let teachers above all explain its theological teaching so that the Sacred Scriptures "may become for the future priests of the Church both a pure and never-failing source for their own spiritual life, as well as food and strength for the sacred task of preaching which they are about to undertake."[30] When they practice the art of criticism, especially so-called literary criticism, let them not pursue it as an end in itself, but that through it they might more plainly perceive the sense intended by God through the sacred writer. Let them not stop, therefore, halfway, content only with their literary discoveries, but show in addition how these things really contribute to a clearer understanding of revealed doctrine, or if it be the case, to the refutation of errors. Instructors who follow these norms will enable their students to find in Sacred Scripture that which can "raise the minds to God, nourish the soul, and further the interior life."[31]

XIII. 4. Those who *instruct the Christian people in sacred sermons* have need of great prudence. Let them above all pass on doctrine, mindful of St. Paul's warning: "Look to yourself and your teaching; hold on to that. For by so doing you will save both yourself and those who listen to you."[32] They are to refrain entirely from pro-

---

28. Irenaeus, *Adversus haereses* 3.1,1 (Harvey 2. 2; *PG* 7. 844).
29. Apostolic Letter, *Quoniam in re biblica* (*EnchBib* §162; *RSS,* 36).
30. *DaS* 55 (*AAS* 35 [1943] 322; *EnchBib* §567; *RSS,* 104).
31. *DaS* 25 (*AAS* 35 [1943] 311; *EnchBib* §552; *R&S,* 93).
32. 1 Tim 4:16.

posing idle or insufficiently established novelties. As for new opinions already solidly established, they may explain them, if need be, but with caution and due care for their listeners. When they narrate biblical events, let them not add imaginative details which are not consonant with the truth.

XIV. This virtue of prudence should be cherished especially *by those who publish for the faithful.* Let them carefully bring forth the heavenly riches of the divine word "that the faithful . . . may be moved and inflamed rightly to conform their lives (to them).[33] They should consider it a sacred duty never to depart in the slightest degree from the common doctrine and tradition of the Church. They should indeed exploit all the real advances of biblical science which the diligence of recent (students) has produced. But they are to avoid entirely the rash remarks of innovators.[34] They are strictly forbidden to disseminate, led on by some pernicious itch for novelty, any trial solutions for difficulties without a prudent selection and serious discrimination, for thus they disturb the faith of many.

XV. This Pontifical Biblical Commission has already considered it proper to recall that books and articles in magazines and newspapers on biblical subjects are subject to the authority and jurisdiction of ordinaries, since they treat of religious matters and pertain to the religious instruction of the faithful.[35] Ordinaries are therefore requested to keep watch with great care over popular writings of this sort.

XVI. 5. Those who are in charge of biblical associations are to comply faithfully with the norms laid down by the Pontifical Biblical Commission.[36]

---

33. *DaS* 50 (*AAS* 35 [1943] 320; *EnchBib* §566; *RSS,* 103).

34. Apostolic Letter, *Quoniam in re biblica* 13 (*EnchBib* §175; *RSS,* 38).

35. Instruction *De consociationibus biblicis* . . . (*AAS* 48 [1956] 63; *EnchBib* §626).

36. Ibid. (*EnchBib* §622–33).

XVII. If all these things are observed, the study of the Sacred Scriptures will contribute to the benefit of the faithful. Even in our time everyone realizes the wisdom of what St. Paul wrote: The sacred writings "can instruct (us) for salvation through faith in Christ Jesus. All Scripture is divinely inspired and profitable for teaching, for reproof, for correction, and for training in uprightness, so that the man of God may be perfect, equipped for every good work."[37]

XVIII. The Holy Father, Pope Paul VI, at the audience graciously granted to the undersigned secretary on 21 April 1964, approved this Instruction and ordered the publication of it.

Rome, 21 April 1964

Secretary of the Commission
Benjamin N. Wambacq O. Praem.

---

37. 2 Tim 3:15–17.

3.

Vatican Council II
Apostolic Constitution, Dei Verbum §19
(*AAS* 58 [1966] 826–27)

Holy Mother the Church has firmly and with utmost constancy held, and continues to hold, that the four Gospels just named, whose historical character the Church unhesitatingly asserts, faithfully hand on what Jesus the Son of God, while living among men, really did and taught for their eternal salvation until the day he was taken up into heaven (see Acts 1:1–2). Indeed, after the ascension of the Lord the apostles handed on to their hearers what he had said and done. This they did with that clearer understanding which they enjoyed[1] after they had been instructed by the events of Christ's risen life [*eventibus gloriosis Christi instructi*] and taught by the light of the Spirit of truth.[2] The sacred authors, however, wrote the four Gospels, selecting some things from the many which had been handed on either by word of mouth or in writing, reducing some of them to a synthesis, explicating [*explanantes* (see Instruction, par. IX)] some things in view of the situation of their churches, and preserving the form of proclamation but always in such fashion that they recounted to us the honest truth about Jesus [*vera et sincera de Iesu*].[3] For their

---

1. See John 2:22; 12:16; cf. 14:26; 16:12–13; 7:39.
2. See John 14:26; 16:13.
3. See the Instruction *Sancta Mater Ecclesia* issued by the Pontifical Commission for the Promotion of Biblical Studies (*AAS* 56 [1964] 712–18, esp. p. 715). Cf. DS §3999b-e. *Sancta Mater Ecclesia* are the first three Latin words with which the Biblical Commission's Instruction begins. Note that "vera et sincera de Iesu" cannot be simply equated with historical truth; see n. 41 above in the commentary on the Instruction.

intention in writing was that either from their own memory and recollections, or from the testimony of those who themselves "from the beginning were eyewitnesses and ministers of the word," we might know "the truth" [*veritatem* (cf. Vulgate version)] concerning those matters about which we have been instructed (cf. Luke 1:2–4).[4]

---

4. In studying this paragraph from Vatican Council II, one must remember that it was the product of much conservative and enlightened debate as *Dei verbum* took shape. The struggle between the two groups of Council fathers can still be seen in the contrast in par. 19 between the unhesitating assertion of the "historical character" of the Gospels and the later nuanced explanation of what the "sacred authors" have passed on to us. This explanation uses phrases derived from the Instruction itself. For a proper understanding of par. 19 and also of par. 11 on inerrancy, one should consult above all A. Grillmeier, "The Divine Inspiration and the Interpretation of Sacred Scripture" (see n. 41 above), 204–15 (especially the details about Form F). Unfortunately, the debate about inerrancy (especially the remarks of Cardinal König and others) has been completely glossed over by such an important Council father as A. Cardinal Bea in his comments on *Dei Verbum* in *The Word of God and Mankind* (Chicago: Franciscan Herald Press, 1967) 184–91. What Bea has written there has to be taken with a grain of salt; it has to yield to what is otherwise known about the Council debate itself.

SELECT BIBLIOGRAPHY

Achtemeier, P. J., *The Inspiration of Scripture: Problems and Proposals* (Philadelphia: Westminster, 1980).

Brown, R. E., *The Critical Meaning of the Bible* (New York: Paulist, 1981).

———, *Jesus God and Man: Modern Biblical Reflections* (Milwaukee: Bruce, 1967).

———, " 'Who Do Men Say That I Am?'—A Survey of Modern Scholarship on Gospel Christology," *Biblical Reflections on Crises Facing the Church* (New York: Paulist, 1975) 20–37.

Conzelmann, H., *Jesus* (Philadelphia: Fortress, 1978).

International Theological Commission, *Select Questions on Christology: September 1980* (Washington, D.C.: United States Catholic Conference, 1980).

Kingsbury, J. D., *Jesus Christ in Matthew, Mark, and Luke* (Philadelphia: Fortress, 1981).

McEleney, N. J., *The Growth of the Gospels* (New York: Paulist, 1979).

Marrow, S. B., *The Words of Jesus in Our Gospels: A Catholic Response to Fundamentalism* (New York: Paulist, 1979).

O'Collins, G., *What Are They Saying About Jesus?* (New York: Paulist, 1977).

N.B. A still more recent image of the Biblical Commission can be seen in a recent publication: *Fede e cultura alla luce della Bibbia: Atti della sessione plenaria 1979 della Pontificia Commissione Biblica* (Turin: Editrice Elle di Ci, 1981). It contains an address of Pope John Paul II to the members of the Commission (26 April 1979) and 15 articles in various languages (English, French, German, Italian, Latin, and Spanish), written by members, and introduced by J.-D. Barthélemy. *Quantum mutata ab illa. . . .*

INDEXES

1

Biblical Index

2

Index of Modern Authors